What people are saying about *Being Fully Present* . . .

Randy's collection of timely personal stories reminds us that "success" in common terms doesn't automatically produce meaning and a well-lived life. Infused with hard-won wisdom, Randy uses his own story to help you find the deeper meaning in your everyday life and work.

His accessible writing style and concise chapters makes this a delightful read: full of wisdom and insight for those of us who want more out of life than a busy calendar and a lucrative career. Reading this book brought me great joy and prompted me to wholeheartedly recommit to the practice of being fully present (this time, equipped with actionable advice from Randy!)

—**Andreas Widmer**, Director, The Arthur and Carlyse Ciocca Center for Principled Entrepreneurship at The Catholic University of America and author of *The Art of Principled Entrepreneurship* and *The Pope & the CEO*

Whenever I'm reading a book, I am panning for gold. Specifically, I am looking for one or two golden nuggets I can sift out of that pan and use in my life to become a better person, a better leader, a better friend. What Randy has written with this book represents a real gift. It is full of many spiritual nuggets that will make you think, challenge you on your faith journey, and spur you on. Randy is one of the finest people I know. This book reinforces that fact. Appreciate and love you, Randy, for who you are and the people you genuinely and faithfully impact!

—**Glen O. Jackson**, Co-founder, Jackson Spalding

Randy Hain practices what he preaches. This book vividly illustrates how he lives his life and is open to serendipitous encounters, making them teaching and learning experiences. It's how life was meant to be—fully present in each moment. Our culture is distracting today. Let's be countercultural. I recommend this book to help you get started.

—**Tim Elmore**, Founder of Growing Leaders, bestselling author, and generational expert

D1545831

Randy has captured an authentic look at the extraordinary moments in an ordinary life. With unassuming depth, he skillfully guides the reader, highlighting the importance of being fully present as well as the importance of reflection in making the most out of our lived experiences. His stories are personal and relatable. The questions at the end of each chapter invite the reader to enter into a space of personal observation and awareness that is foundational in connecting with our deepest self and opens the door for growth and development.

—**Carla María Molina,** Catholic Executive Coach and President of Executive Solutions

In *Being Fully Present*, Randy Hain weaves another tapestry of wisdom that will keep you eagerly turning the pages. In a world where distractions abound, this book serves as a poignant reminder to treasure life's encounters—from serendipitous meetings to heartfelt conversations with those we hold dear. Whether you're seeking personal growth, deeper connections, or simply a captivating read, this book not only delivers but also enriches your perspective on life.

—**Darin W. White**, PhD, Margaret Gage Bush Distinguished Professor and Executive Director, Center for Sports Analytics at Samford University

The three greatest gifts we can give another human being are to be present, listening for meaning and asking great and relevant questions. My good friend Randy Hain asks the reader to reflect on their own lives with the intention of bringing more of these great gifts into their lives and the lives of those that matter most to them.

—**Ray V. Padrón**, Partner, Advisor, and Former CEO of Brightworth Wealth Management

Randy Hain writes in such an authentic manner that each chapter makes you immensely introspective. He uses his stories to help you calibrate your priorities and take stock on where you spend your time and energy. I left this book with a wonderful feeling of hope and opportunity.

—**Ben Milsom**, former NFL executive, transformational people leader, husband, father, coach, and community servant

Randy Hain's newest book, *Being Fully Present*, builds beautifully on the foundation he laid with his popular 2022 release *Upon Reflection*. He takes the reader through a series of true stories from his life that will at times deeply move you and at other times reveal the powerful lessons Randy so capably draws from everyday life. As a longtime friend and colleague of Randy, Randy's vulnerability and authenticity comes through masterfully as he shares insights into his faith, family, challenges, and the most important life lessons he has learned over the years. I strongly recommend *Being Fully Present* and promise you will be inspired and motivated to adopt the helpful practices and ideas sewn throughout this gem of a book.

—**Brandon Smith**, President of The Worksmiths, Co-founder of the Leadership Foundry, and author of *The Hot Sauce Principle* and *The Author vs Editor Dilemma*

Randy continues to inspire and motivate! You can read *Being Fully Present* in one sitting—but I assure you that you will flag pages and chapters to come back to for further reflection. Randy includes prompts after each of his stories that made me think about my everyday life choices and events just a little differently. I have been striving to be present in my life for years now; Randy's book is just the spark I needed to remind me how important it is to be present, to be aware, and to seek love in all we do. Highly recommend reading this book, either on your own or within a trusted small group!

—**Amelia Fox**, Chief Strategy Officer and Chief of Staff for Lutheran Services Florida

In a time where it might seem as though our core values have been relegated to the background, besieged, or even entirely forgotten, Randy Hain brings them back to the forefront in his newest book, *Being Fully Present*. Each chapter of the book imparts a beautiful life lesson, easily overlooked by those who are not fully engaged in the present moment. Randy challenges readers to examine their lives and adopt a new perspective, asking: "How can I grow from this situation? What can I learn?" This, after all, lies at the heart of human connection, an area for which Randy is widely recognized. If we are constantly too busy or too distracted, we risk missing out on the simple pleasures of life. And without adversity, how can we truly appreciate the nature of joy and savor each moment? In this book, Randy gives practical examples and thoughtful prompts we can apply to our very own lives to discover the gold within.

—**Whitney Mendoza**, Partner, Fifth City and Company

Life can move fast if we let it. Randy Hain reminds us that being fully present means slowing down so we don't miss the best parts of life. As an ambitious type, I often feel the pull of "not enough time." Reading *Being Fully Present* was a beautiful blessing serving as the reminder I needed to see the beauty of the here and now and truly focus on the real priority of life. Randy's collection of stories will touch your heart and lead you to where you've been searching . . . if you are open to it.

—**Ellen Twomey**, Managing Director of Fugitive Labs, Mother, Wife, and Friend

In *Being Fully Present*, Randy Hain delivers insightful stories for how to fully engage with those around you and to find the "gold nuggets" of each moment regardless of the situation. Hain's vulnerability and transparency will encourage and challenge you to be more authentic in the workplace by not checking your faith at the office door. You will find yourself smiling, nodding, and embracing the truths of each story and then seeking ways to apply the message. Highly recommend this book!

—**John Riordan**, CEO of Harvest Technology Group

There is a lot of talk these days about mindfulness, being unplugged, and truly being present in the moment, not only with others, but also with ourselves. Randy has collected a treasure of honest and thought-provoking experiences that we can all relate to in our daily lives. For some, these stories may be heartwarming, for some insightful, and for others, a wake-up call. I especially enjoyed the questions at the end of each chapter that challenged me to honestly reflect on my own life. These questions form a road map to help us learn where to mine for gold in our everyday encounters. Whether you are a person of faith or not, you will become aware that there are no real coincidences in life. Our lives are shaped by every person God places in our path, if we will only take a quiet moment to peek below the surface for the lessons to be revealed.

—**Laurie Ann Stetzer**, Managing Partner of Loric Consulting

After surviving a global pandemic which redefined social conventions by forcing us to isolation and making us more aware of our own mortality and the fragility of life, it was not uncommon to feel alone, depressed, anxious, and confused about how to approach life with cautious optimism. In this timely book, Randy reminds us of the importance of finding peace and joy in the ordinary interactions God puts in our path every day. Too often we allow our big-picture goals, the pursuit of success both personally and professionally, life challenges, and external noise to occupy our minds to the point of missing out on the opportunities we have to learn and to make a positive impact in the lives around us every single moment of the day. We are not meant to live our lives without God's help, and through his own experiences, Randy shows us practical ways to make our entire day an ongoing conversation with God and to develop an ear for His whisper—as with Elijah at Mount Horeb (1 Kings 19:11–13).

—**Ricardo Alvarado**, Consulting Executive

The real teacher in life is the experience of life itself. Author Randy Hain does not miss out on this experience, and his eloquent accounts of the mini miracles that have resulted in "epiphanies and powerful lessons" remind all of us to turn our attention to the miraculous moments occurring in our own lives each day. They are fleeting, subtle—and without presence we surely miss them.

Keep a copy on your nightstand and read a story when you need to close your day with gratitude or start it with inspiration. Keep a copy on your kitchen table and read a story aloud to family members after a meal. Hain closes each story with reflection questions perfect for personal journaling or meaningful discussions with friends and loved ones. *Being Fully Present* is a treasure chest of wisdom and points to what's important in a world filled with distractions.

—**Andrea Chilcote**, Founder and CEO of Morningstar Ventures and Author of *What Leaders Need Now*

As a busy executive, I must constantly fight to make time for reading and reflection. It's aggravating after fighting for that precious time to be disappointed by sound-bite seeking titles or works that otherwise fall short. Randy Hain's books are different, because Randy is different. I've come to know Randy as a deeply reflective, humble, faith-filled, insightful man and leader. His previous works are favorites of mine to return to again and again. With *Being Fully Present*, Randy adds to his consistently thought-provoking wisdom and effective writing style with an intense and inspiringly personal work, reminding us of what truly matters. Hain has shared with readers here a profound and beautiful glimpse at the eminently relatable lives and events that have turned his life for the better. His reflection questions after each short chapter are perfect for self-reflection or group and family sharing. These stories will encourage you, challenge you, and in some cases, even sting a little—maybe even a lot. I'm grateful for all of them.

—**Doran Oancia**, President and CEO of CHEMEX Global and Fellow Sojourner

I enjoyed this book the most of all Randy's publications. Much as Anthony DeMello suggested we do in his book, Randy has looked at himself from the outside, and shared what he has learned from this deep introspection. He extracts so much from everyday life events, and in so doing has encouraged me to look deeper at my own daily experiences. Powerful!

—**Anthony Lynch**, Founder and President of
Thoughtful Partners

Being Fully Present by Randy Hain is not just a book of lovely stories and reflections; it is a call to all of us to be more present at work as well as in our personal lives. What makes this book great is how Randy gives you the tools to be more present. It is a guide to better relationships with everyone in your life . . . a powerful guide that works!

—**Chester Elton**, Bestselling Author of *The Carrot Principle* and
Leading with Gratitude

Being Fully Present is a beautifully written book of faith-filled stories and anecdotes of Randy Hain's blessed life. *Being Fully Present* challenged me to find opportunities to slow down and enjoy the simple yet meaningful moments in my life. His stories and examples are relatable while creating a compelling case to reflect and take the time to enjoy God's blessings in every part of our lives. This is a much-needed book in a society where everything feels hectic, urgent, and reactive. I highly recommend it!

—**Ash Merchant**, Founder and CEO of Lionheart Partners

In his most recent book, *Being Fully Present: True Stories of Epiphanies and Powerful Lessons from Everyday Life*, author Randy Hain shares a collection of very personal stories drawn from his life. These vignettes feature lessons gleaned from encounters with his family, friends, strangers, and business associates. He often draws upon his strong Catholic faith as he seeks to gain wisdom, though one need not be Catholic to benefit greatly from this book. Through these delightful stories, the author demonstrates and then invites the reader to engage in meaningful self-reflection.

Readers who are open to a spiritual journey will find that this book encourages and guides them to be less distracted by the noise in the world. The book coaches the readers to build stronger relationships by being better observers of people and better listeners. A key theme woven throughout is that this can be best brought out when one prioritizes time spent based on being fully present to others.

This book, while entertaining from a human-interest point of view, goes a big step further in that it invites the reader on a deep journey of self-discovery through being fully present to the world around them. Thank you, Randy Hain, for sharing your wisdom through this insightful and helpful book!

—**Sara Perlaky FitzGerald**, PhD, Former Director of Sales and Marketing @ Cytiva, Special Needs Mom, and lifelong Catholic

Randy Hain has given us gold once again. His particular references to reflection, engagement, and "mining for gold" are spot-on in this busy and easily distracted world in which we live. His storytelling is unique and genuine, his solutions and strategies are meaningful and practical, and his thoughts are grounded and shared through the filter of his strong faith.

—**Patrick McNulty**, Retired Senior Business and Nonprofit Leader

BEING FULLY PRESENT

True Stories of Epiphanies and Powerful Lessons from Everyday Life

Randy Hain

Author of *Essential Wisdom for Leaders of Every Generation*

SERVIAM PRESS

ISBN: 978-1-7377244-4-5   (softcover)
ISBN 978-1-7377244-6-9   (hardcover)
ISBN: 978-1-7377244-5-2   (e-book)

Published by Serviam Press, LLC
www.serviampress.com

This book is dedicated with love and gratitude to my wonderful wife, Sandra.

CONTENTS

INTRODUCTION

A friend of mine who read an early version of this book asked me what "being fully present" meant to me. It is a great question, and the way I think about it is fundamentally core to understanding the point of this new book. As I have grown older, more experienced, and hopefully a little wiser, I've come to recognize the importance of being fully present and truly experiencing the value of a conversation or situation. This requires me to not be distracted, to actively listen, to ask relevant questions, and to look below the surface for deeper meanings I should glean from the moment.

Being fully present does not always have to involve meeting with another person. There are a number of stories in this book when I take you back to a powerful memory, my observations of others or situations when I am alone in prayer . . . I even share a fable about an encounter with my future self. To me, being fully present is about being fully alert and keenly aware of others or the situation at hand. It is about deriving powerful lessons you are meant to learn in that moment or possibly later after reflection. It is also about thoughtfully discerning how you might best be able to help others.

In my last book, *Upon Reflection: Helpful Insights and Timeless Lessons for the Busy Professional*, I shared a collection of practical and thought-provoking ideas that were largely derived from my own practice of thoughtful reflection. Each chapter represented, in some way, the fruit of the practice of reflection and covered a host of topics relevant and helpful for today's professional. Perhaps because of the challenging state of the world and the hectic pace many of us keep, it seemed to resonate with readers in a special way and is one of my favorites from the ten books I have written over the years.

My newest work, *Being Fully Present: True Stories of Epiphanies and Powerful Lessons from Everyday Life*, is perhaps one of the most personal books I have written. This is definitely not a business book, but I am clearly a business professional dealing with life's challenges throughout the pages you are about to read. I have pulled together more than twenty brief and eclectic stories from the last two decades of my life that highlight the value of being fully present in a number of situations and the gifts, epiphanies and lessons I have derived from truly living in the moment without distractions. I place a premium on authenticity, and the stories in this book are all real life situations, often involving my faith and family.

If you are a person of faith, curious about faith, or have no faith at all, I invite you to read, appreciate, and hopefully enjoy this book. I engage every day with people who do not share my beliefs or worldview, but I try very hard to meet people where they are with respect, kindness, and an openness to learn. I would respectfully ask the same of the readers of this book.

One of the central themes of *Being Fully Present* is the importance of the "encounter." Sometimes, this encounter is with a random person I meet or someone close to me and the powerful lessons I derived from a simple conversation. Some of the encounters are memories of profound moments in my life or of someone no longer with us. There are stories of epiphanies and life-changing events where the only viable explanation is God at work. One of my favorite types of encounter, which is frequently featured in this book, is the person or people who come into my life at exactly the right time with some epiphany or lesson I need to learn.

My sincere desire for you after finishing this book is that you will slow down, pay attention, and spend more time being fully present. I hope you'll spend less time looking at screens and more time listening, talking, thinking, praying, and reflecting. I encourage you to savor every conversation, be open every minute of every day to epiphanies waiting to be revealed, look for "God wink" moments that will change your life, and revisit powerful memories to see what you may have missed. Also, I encourage you to look for opportunities when you are fully present to have a positive impact on others.

I hope what you read here inspires you, challenges you, opens the aperture of your thinking, and motivates you to make changes if necessary. In my life, the practice of being fully present, followed by thoughtful reflection, has usually led to some sort of needed course correction that helped me get back on track. The stories in this book have helped shape me in countless ways, and I hope they'll do the same for you.

CHAPTER 1

A Courageous Young Man

I recently reflected on a Sunday Mass several years ago when I had an opportunity to witness a very special moment at my parish. An eighteen-year-old young man with high-functioning autism was taking his first turn as a lector. The lector role is an important one with serious responsibility, but this young man showed confidence and little fear as he read a very long Scripture passage from Exodus to the several hundred people in attendance. The compliments he received from countless well-wishers after Mass for the great job he did brought a shy smile to his face as he basked in the glow of the kind words shared by his fellow parishioners.

This is a heartwarming story to be sure, but there is more here than meets the eye. There was a small army of loving and caring people in the parish who trained, supported, encouraged, and prayed for him to get to this wonderful moment of personal success on that Sunday morning. The names might not mean anything to you, but people like Jeanne, Monsignor Peter, Deacon Scott, Deacon Mike, Sue, and others who helped him are the ones who have modeled the very best of what it means to be Catholic. They represent in their actions and words the elements of a caring family so critical for a thriving parish community.

The young man's mother, father, and younger brother looked both anxious and proud as they watched him achieve this brief moment of triumph. What did this mean to them? Did his parents envision that this day was possible in the early years after his diagnosis with autism when a normal future for their son looked bleak? How few are little victories like this in families with special needs children! These parents must long for an opportunity to see their oldest child excel in life and receive accolades for achievements that other families may sometimes take for granted.

I was deeply touched by the courage of the young man for even attempting such a thing. Knowing something about autism, I realize the incredible effort he had to make to do something many of us would have seen as easy or routine. Nothing is easy for children or adults on the autism spectrum, and they often struggle to fit in to a world they find alien and sometimes hostile. His example has inspired me, and it has already helped me be more sensitive to other people I encounter each day with the great burdens they may have on their shoulders. I pray I never take for granted the things I can do that others cannot.

This special young man is named Alex, and I know him well because . . . he is my son.

My wife and I are blessed beyond measure to be his parents, and we are very proud of our oldest child. Maybe, just maybe, the breakthrough he had that Sunday will be one of many in the years to come. We pray that a future we once saw as limited by autism will be blessed by God to bear much fruit for Alex, for those who love him, and for the people he encounters in his life.

Have you experienced special moments like this in your life? How did these moments or individuals inspire you to be a better person? How have you changed because of them?

CHAPTER 2

Practicing Acceptance and Seeing Burdens as Blessings

Many years ago, one Sunday after Mass, one of our priests asked me and my wife how he could pray for our family. We asked him to pray, as we frequently did, for our oldest son's future and that he be healed of his autism. He looked at us thoughtfully for a moment and then shared some guidance with us that has been the ongoing catalyst for a great deal of conversation and reflection in our home since that time. He encouraged us to stop praying for healing and pray instead for *acceptance*.

Let me explain.

He said there was nothing wrong with asking God to heal our son. But we first needed to ask for the ability to fully accept the beautiful gift of our child *exactly as God created him*. By asking for healing first, we were in essence asking God to improve on His creation without first understanding the lessons and blessings His gift has provided our family. We have always viewed our oldest son as a blessing and know we could not possibly love him more than we do now. But we may have mistaken love for acceptance as we continued to pray over the years for God to remake him into our vision of a well-formed and healthy child. We had somewhat selfishly asked God to redo His handiwork when we should have been accepting of God's plan for his life and trusting that the Father who loves us wants only what is best for him.

> If you follow the will of God, you know that in spite of all the terrible things that happen to you, you will never lose a final refuge. You know that the foundation of the world is love, so that even when no human being can or will help you, you may go on, trusting in the One that loves you.
> —Pope Emeritus Benedict XVI, *Jesus of Nazareth*

Acknowledging this has been both humbling and illuminating as I think about how to apply "acceptance" into other areas of my life. This period of reflection has made me realize how often without thinking I ask God for His help in improving situations and solving problems. Instead of praying for acceptance and discernment about what lessons God wants to teach me or the blessings hidden in these challenges, I seek to reshape the issues into something more pleasing to me instead of pleasing to Him.

- Do you ever fall into the "acceptance trap" as well?
- Do you see career setbacks as learning opportunities to help you grow and learn?
- Do you see opportunities for spiritual growth in our emotional struggles and financial setbacks?
- Does illness (yours or others) offer opportunities to turn suffering into a blessing?

As St. Paul says, "I consider that the sufferings of this present time are as nothing compared with the glory to be revealed for us" (Romans 8:18). It is often difficult to see the blessings and good in any kind of suffering, yet we know from Church teaching there is redemptive power in suffering if we learn to give it up to God. Practicing acceptance may require a radical recalibration of our mindsets as well as complete trust and faith in God's plan for our lives. We must be faithful, humble, patient, obedient and prayerful if we are to learn the lessons and blessings God has in store for us in our daily trials. We must also seek to glorify Him and not ourselves through the way we deal with challenges and always express our gratitude for the good *and* bad that comes our way.

> We always find that those who walked closest to Christ were those who had to bear the greatest trials.
>
> —St. Teresa of Avila

I can look back now and see the tremendous positive influence our oldest son has had on our family. His diagnosis with autism more than twenty-four years ago and the challenges this presented began the long and often difficult process of lowering the wall around my closed-off heart. In the summer of 2005, we moved into the area in which we now live to be closer to his school and therapists. This move began a chain of events that eventually led to our family joining the Catholic Church the following year. The opening of my heart which began at his diagnosis allowed me to experience a profound conversion experience in September

2005 when I finally surrendered to Christ and put aside the pride and stubbornness that had dominated my life for so long. Without a doubt, our gifted child and his presence in our lives was a significant catalyst behind our joining the Catholic Church and the strong faith our family has today.

Maybe this was God's plan all along for our son, and I know my wife and I were specifically chosen out of all the parents in the world to be his parents. I am just grateful that I can see it now and accept him, not only as one of my wonderful children who I love, but also as a child of God who was given to us for His divine purpose.

Perhaps in this crazy world in which we live, we can all more thoughtfully practice acceptance of God's will and see the challenges in our lives as blessings, not burdens.

Heavenly Father, I humbly ask that you grant me the gift of acceptance today. Please help me to understand the lessons and blessings hidden within the challenges my family and I will face and know that I am grateful to you for our lives and the incredible gift and sacrifice of your son Jesus Christ. Amen.

How does this idea of acceptance speak to you? In your own life, do you possibly have an opportunity to accept and appreciate your own difficult circumstances and challenges as blessings and learning experiences instead of burdens?

CHAPTER 3

Joy, Encouragement, and a Mother's Love

One of the earliest memories I have of my mother, Sandi, is when I was three or four years old. It was during summer, and we were living in our first home in Annapolis, Maryland. I remember playing in the front yard with my mother and feeling very happy and safe. I recall vividly the expression on her face—she radiated joy, encouragement, and a mother's love all in a simple look which has long been captured in my mind. Joy, encouragement, and love . . . these are words that evoke warm feelings in me, and they accurately describe how she lived her life.

There are many other memories of my mother, too many to share here. What strikes me, as I cast my thoughts to the past, is that throughout her life, in good times and bad and through triumph and tragedy, she was always a consistent and positive influence for me and countless others. She was forever joyful, encouraging, and loving.

Although she grew up in a challenging home, my mother chose to be a loving and devoted wife and mother.

My mother always credited her faith as her lifeline and the catalyst for the good but tough choices she made in her life. For as long as I can remember, she was a devout Christian, and her relationship with Christ sustained and molded her in ways which were obvious to all who knew her. I know in my heart that as soon as she entered Heaven, she heard Christ say, "Well done, good and faithful servant."

My mother worked her entire adult life until illness forced her to retire. I recall that we didn't have a lot of extras when I was growing up, but she saw to it that we had what we needed. We had quality family time over dinner every night. My sister and I learned the value of hard work from both of our parents, especially my mother, as she had a full-time job as well as the more important roles of wife and mom. She played all of these roles joyfully and without complaint. My mother also saw to it that we had love in our house, encouragement to do our best, and a focus on faith that was best taught to us by her own shining example.

"How can I help?" and "I will pray for you" were often among the first words out of her mouth to friends, family and strangers alike, and everyone knew she meant it. I am amazed at the number of lives my mother deeply touched, including my own. She was an inspiration to others through her friendship, mentoring, writing, caregiving and, one of her favorite roles, Sunday School Teacher.

In many ways I am my father's son. As a husband and father, much of who I am and what I do has been influenced by his example. But as I grow older, I am grateful that I have learned to appreciate my heart—a heart I received from my mother. I am now in my fifties, and with each passing year, I feel more strongly the influence of her life on my own. My own efforts to help and encourage others are in many ways shaped by her lifetime of selfless service. I am incredibly grateful for her influence, but I have a long way to go to emulate her loving and generous example. I pray that my sons will remember the lessons they learned from their Nana as well.

I wrote much of this reflection at thirty thousand feet on a flight to Tampa to see my mother in the hospital a few weeks before her health started to seriously decline. Long flights in airplanes are wonderful opportunities for deep thinking, and that particular trip was cathartic and a true blessing for me as I played the movie of my mother's life over and over in my head. I'm grateful I had the opportunity to read this reflection to her while she was still with us.

In the final days of her life, with her family near her and an endless parade of friends visiting her, she had a chance to say her goodbyes and reflect on her life. One of the last things my mother said to me was that she hoped people would remember her life and not just the last days of her illness. As for me, I will always see her, as I did over fifty years ago, smiling at me with joy, encouragement, and a mother's love.

Sandi Hain passed away on February 22, 2010, after a long illness, surrounded by family and friends who loved her.

Think about the lives of loved ones you hold most dear? What was their impact on your life? What are you doing to keep their memories alive?

CHAPTER 4

The Paradox of Help

Many years ago, a friend shared a candid observation over coffee one morning, and it had a profound effect on me. "Randy, I have noticed that you really enjoy helping people," he said, "but you seem uncomfortable when people try to help you. By not allowing them the opportunity to help, you are denying them the very grace you receive from God when you help them." My friend's keen observation and fraternal correction stopped me in my tracks, and the conversation has stayed with me over the years.

Years of growing self-awareness has helped me understand that I do sometimes struggle to let people help me. I have been uncomfortable with this since I was a teenager. My practice of reaching out first with an offer of help to the people I encountered allowed me to maintain a protective barrier around my heart and retain some measure of control. I have always genuinely found pleasure in helping others, but I have recognized over the years that I was also serving a subtle need to maintain some emotional distance between me and others. I have often observed similar discomfort in others, especially men, with receiving help. Why do we sometimes struggle in this area? Conversations with people who I felt were similarly challenged and my own self-reflection have led me to the following potential causes:

- **Pride.** We may be stubbornly avoiding assistance from others because of the sin of pride. "Do I need help? No thanks. I am doing great!"
- **Lack of Emotional Intelligence.** We may not pick up on someone else's genuine desire to help us or we may misunderstand their motivation.
- **Fear of Exposure.** We don't want to expose our flaws or problems to others and be seen as less than perfect.
- **"One Up" Syndrome.** For some of us, there may be a desire to have people in our debt and not the other way around. This is wrong on many levels! Help should always be given freely and accepted graciously . . . with no expectation of return from either side.
- **Lack of Self-Awareness.** We may not know ourselves and our own challenges well enough to realize we have a problem or understand how to allow others to help us.

The chapter thus far has focused on why we may struggle to receive help from others. The next logical question is this: *What are we denying others when we are not accepting of their help?* My friend pointed out that I was denying others the opportunity to receive God's grace by my discomfort with receiving help. People offering unsolicited help or hoping to return our kind assistance may simply be acting out of generosity and love. Others may desire to help us out of a desire to restore their own poor self-esteem or overcome low self-confidence and might see their offer of assistance to us as a way to feel "normal" again.

I often see this in people experiencing job transition. It may seem counterintuitive, but I encourage all of us to seek out friends, family or anyone we encounter who is struggling with some challenge and consider asking them for help. I am sure we all have plenty of room for help in our lives! Plus, don't we all stand a little taller and straighter when someone asks us for assistance? For many, this simple act of love and kindness from us just might make their day.

A lot of thoughtful reflection, accountability from trusted friends, and a sincere desire to change have helped me largely overcome my "help issues," although I am still far from perfect. I have learned to not only more easily accept assistance, but to seek it out for those needing help in my extended network. It is now much more comfortable to ask for prayers for my family, job search help or introductions for a friend in need, support for my favorite nonprofits, or help in passing along the word about my latest book.

If you are reading this and feeling convicted, know there is a path forward to change if you are willing to be humble and recognize the gift you are giving to others when you receive help from them.

Do you find it difficult to receive help? Why?
Did any of the causes listed above resonate with you?
How can you go out of your way in the days ahead to intentionally let someone help you, even in a small way?

CHAPTER 5

He Had a Great Career

What you are about to read is a fable of sorts about a man who had it all, yet he wasn't fulfilled. It's a story of misplaced priorities, wasted opportunities, heartbreak, forgiveness, love, and ultimately, redemption. A familiar tale, perhaps, but it goes like this . . .

The sun shone brightly that September morning as the brothers stood next to the grave of their late father. Just a few minutes before, they had been surrounded by family and their father's business friends, and their ears had been filled with the kind words of Father Benton, their parish priest. The words of praise about their father's life left them feeling empty and uncomfortable as they stared at the coffin in the ground.

"I can only say this to you, but I don't know how I should feel right now," Mike declared to Greg as they walked back to their car. "Dad spent our entire lives on an airplane, chained to his office or playing golf with his buddies on the weekend. I feel like we didn't even know him. I know this sounds selfish, but I feel cheated!"

Greg put his hand on his brother's shoulder. "Come

on, Mike! he said. "It wasn't that bad. Dad had a lot of responsibility. He took good care of the family, and we never lacked for anything. He would have been around more if he could."

"Greg, you have always defended him, even when you hurt as much as I did when he missed our baseball games and Cub Scout camping trips. He even missed your high school graduation because of business! What about Mom? How did she feel all those years? Did you see her sobbing on Aunt Mary's shoulder during the funeral? I wonder what she's thinking about the future now that Dad is gone. We'd better get over to Aunt Mary's for the reception and look in on her."

The brothers were lost in their own conflicting thoughts as they drove to their aunt's home. Sadness . . . regret . . . and perhaps a little bitterness dominated their emotions as they joined the large crowd inside. There were hugs and sympathetic comments, and quite a few people encouraged them not to be sad and instead celebrate their father's life . . . which only made things worse in light of their recent conversation.

Then their mother beckoned them to join her in Aunt Mary's guest room upstairs.

"Boys, we need to talk, and we haven't had much time for that since your father's heart attack. The last few days have been a blur for me, and I can only imagine what this has been like for you."

Mike spoke first, "Mom, Greg and I have been trying to wrestle with all of this, and it's hard. Since we have been in college, we have been even more distant than usual from

Dad, other than the occasional phone call and holiday visits home. I know everyone expects us to be crying right now, but we can't help but remember a father who seemed to care more about his job than about us. Maybe that's not fair, but that's how we feel."

Tears welled up in their mother's eyes as she hugged her sons and asked them to sit down. "I know how hard it was for you growing up, and I tried my best to compensate for your father's hectic life. Your dad was a good man, and he felt he was doing the right things for our family. But there was a recent change in him you weren't aware of. Over the last few months, your father started going to Mass with me again. We also had a few short conversations recently about his desire to do things differently with the rest of his life, and I could tell he had a heavy heart. He was coming to some big decision points about his life. Here's something I found next to the computer in your dad's study the morning after he passed away. Greg, will you please read this aloud for us?"

Greg nervously took the pages from his mother's hand and saw a typewritten letter to him and his brother from their father. It was dated September 12—the day before he was found dead of a heart attack on the running trail near his office. Greg began reading . . .

September 12, 2011
Dear Mike and Greg,

I look forward to seeing you both during your Thanksgiving break from school. I have never written you boys before, so this may appear a little strange to you. My intention is to share a few important things that have been on my mind lately and discuss them when we are all together again.

I have been reflecting a lot lately on my life and the kind of husband and father I have been. It is probably no surprise to you that I give myself a failing grade. I realize very clearly that I have not been there for you and your mother over the years. It is easy to justify and rationalize our actions, and I have done that for years. I convinced myself that our big house, nice cars, great vacations, and the lifestyle I provided for us was worth my slavish devotion to my career. I thought this justified all of my absences and the sacrifices I forced our family to make over the years. I now realize that I was wrong.

Your mother is a saint, and she deserved much more from me in our twenty-four years of marriage. I have always loved your mother very much, but I rarely told her and thought I was showing her my love by providing a great lifestyle. I was a fool, and I am committed to making it up to her. She has been the bedrock of our family, and you boys are who you are because of your mother's great influence.

Greg . . . Mike . . . I owe you a sincere apology for not being there over the years. I really mean it. I have come to realize that all the stuff we have is worthless compared to the lost opportunities to be a meaningful part of your lives. I hope you will forgive me and give me another chance when we sit down at Thanksgiving.

I am hopeful that in the years ahead we will become closer—the way a family should be. I want to rediscover my Catholic faith and experience the joy I have seen in your mother's eyes when she talks about her own faith journey or attends Mass. Serving in the community and giving back to others is also high on my list of new priorities.

I want you to promise me something: Please learn from my example! Be a better father, husband, and steward of your gifts than I was and don't waste the years ahead of you. I wish someone had gotten my attention when I was much younger and helped me not waste the greatest years of my life. I hope to do that for you in the years ahead.

I have seen the light, and I hope to make amends. Again, please find it in your hearts to forgive me.

I truly love you more than you can ever know.

Dad

Tears were streaming down all their faces. Greg and Mike hugged their mother as the anger and resentment they had felt gave way to genuine grief.

Mike spoke first. "I only wish we had time to have that Thanksgiving together—to truly get to know each other and start over. I would have liked to have known the man who wrote this letter."

Greg was clutching the pages tightly as he whispered, "We need to pray for Dad and also pray that we will learn from his mistakes and pass these lessons on to our own children. It's strange that at the gravesite I thought his headstone should have read, 'He Had a Great Career' and now I want it to say, 'Loving Father and Husband' to honor his dramatic change of heart."

Their mother responded, "Boys, please don't wait until the end of your lives to make amends. I have no doubt that your father would have done what he said, but you can't wait like he did. Start living today like it is the last day of your lives."

—The End—

Some of us may know someone like the man in this tale and the unintentional misguided priorities he or she pursued in their lives. I know this character very well because . . . *I am the father in this story.* Let me explain. In December 1999, I left a very successful career as the Vice President of People for a national billion-dollar restaurant chain, where I was responsible for the company's recruiting, training, and diversity efforts. As a thirty-two-year old senior leader of the company, I had significant responsibility, the respect of my peers, and a bright future ahead of me. But as much as I loved the work, I was miserable.

I traveled three weeks out of every month for four years. I worked most weekends and put in around seventy to eighty hours a week. As a member of the senior leadership team, I was expected to be in the restaurants on every major holiday to set a good example. That does not mesh well with a young family. I saw my infant son growing up before my eyes while I was barely present. My wife and I were growing distant because of my workaholic tendencies and the demands of my job. I looked around me and saw many of my peers having marital problems or already divorced.

I made a conscious decision to leave this organization and get my life back on track. I was being pursued at that time by a national executive search firm and was drawn to the opportunity and the work/life balance it offered. The great company culture and strong values of the leadership team were also very appealing. I made a decision to join the new company, shocking everyone who knew me. Many thought I was committing career suicide, but I knew I was saving my family and embarking on the pursuit of a life filled with meaning. The years since have validated my decision in positive ways I could never have imagined.

Why did I title this chapter "He Had a Great Career"? I often wonder what would have happened if I had never left my old employer in 1999, and simply looked a decade or so into the future. This tragic story could have easily been my own story if I had not made some critical decisions about work, family, faith and life. My own tombstone could have sadly read, "He Had a Great Career," and that would have been a tragic outcome and wasted opportunity to lead a much more fulfilling life.

Are your priorities in the right order? What big decisions about your life and career do you need to make right now? What is keeping you from making them?

CHAPTER 6

Being Grateful for . . .
My Challenges?

Do you ever struggle to feel grateful? I remember one morning not long ago waking up in a "mood." Maybe it was the stress of having too much on my plate as I pondered my numerous family and work commitments. Perhaps it was the anxiety around growing my business in a difficult economy. It may have been the stress around giving my sons all they need from me as a father in these critical years of their lives. It could have been my frustration with the state of political discourse in our country. It's quite possible I just needed a break and some alone time in prayer.

I drove to our parish chapel with the hope of finding peace, quiet, and my lost gratitude. Instead, all I could do was dwell on my challenges and how frustrated I was with my inability to calm my mind. I struggled to feel grateful for my blessings. Finally, I prayed an Our Father and left . . . feeling worse than when I entered the chapel.

As I drove away, it hit me: I was expressing gratitude for the wrong things. I was trying to be grateful for all of my blessings, but I felt nothing. I decided to instead be grateful for my challenges. That's right . . . *my challenges*. If I was not having a good day, maybe God was trying to teach me something and I needed to be attentive to the lesson. As I prayed about each of my challenges, I began to see what I was supposed to learn—and a genuine feeling of gratitude began to creep into my heart.

My overflowing plate was a reminder to be thankful for meaningful work which I love and to be a better steward of my time. My oldest son has challenges, but I am most grateful that he is my special child and a blessing in our lives. My younger son, learning to make his way after college, needs me to be a better listener and a candid guide in this stage of his life. My wife needs me to be more present and go all the way each day, not just meet her halfway. Finally, I began to see my busy calendar as numerous opportunities to serve the countless people Christ places before me each day and to be more grateful that I am blessed to serve Him by helping others.

It's easy to focus only on the good and the easy blessings when expressing gratitude. It's also easy to allow ourselves to gripe when things are not going well. For me, this epiphany was a profound lesson on the need to be grateful for my challenges and the lessons they contain. Our earthly journey is not an easy one, and there will be difficulties and even suffering. Our response to these challenges makes all the difference.

Do you ever struggle with gratitude? How might you express gratitude for the difficult things in your life? What lessons and blessings could they contain?

BEING GRATEFUL FOR . . . MY CHALLENGES?

Pause for a minute and think of two challenges in your life. Think, discern, and pray about the good these struggles may contain and express gratitude for them.

CHAPTER 7

The Good Samaritan within All of Us

Are you frustrated with the current state of the world? It's difficult to get through the day without feeling overwhelmed by the onslaught of bad news on the economy, dysfunctional government, rising crime—the list is endless. It is incredibly rare for the media to show the positive and uplifting stories we all hope are out there but do not often see. Well, I have one for you.

As I have shared in previous chapters of this book, my oldest son has high-functioning autism. You may know that people on the autism spectrum often deal with a host of challenges around living independently, interacting with others, and making friends. Parents of children with autism often feel like they live in an isolated vacuum and wonder if anybody really understands how difficult their lives can be.

My wife received a call several years ago when Alex was entering his teen years from a friend in our neighborhood who has had enormous struggles of her own. At that time, she had just fought her way back from a life-threatening illness, and her husband had lost his job a few months before. This woman would have every justifiable reason to retreat from the world, focus on her own problems, and not worry about her neighbors. But she was *different*. This woman was a true Good Samaritan, because she called to ask if our son would like a job watering her plants and collecting her mail while her family was on vacation that summer. I don't think she had ever spent meaningful time with our son, but she knew about him from my wife and our church community. She was able to look past her own significant problems and show unbelievable kindness to our son. I can't tell you how overwhelmed my wife and I felt at her generosity. I get teary-eyed at the thought of it.

This may not seem like a big deal to you, but our son never had a job before. He had never been responsible for anything outside of school or our home. He had certainly never earned money for any sort of work. For one week that summer, our son was like the other kids who had summer jobs. He felt important, responsible, and needed. He felt the satisfaction of using money he earned to buy something he wanted. My wife and I began to feel the cautious hope that someday, other generous Good Samaritans like our neighbor would look beyond their own struggles and extend opportunities to our son as he makes his way in the world. What an incredible gift this kind lady gave our family.

I share this brief story with you as an encouragement that we all have a Good Samaritan somewhere deep within us. It is easy to get lost in our own problems, but we have significant opportunities every day to reach out to people around us who may be struggling. Our neighbor was able to look beyond her own challenges and demonstrate a random act of incredible kindness to our son.

I wonder . . . who can you and I help today?

Reflect on the people you know for a moment. Who is struggling right now? Despite your own challenges, what could you do to make a positive difference in their lives this week? It could be a word of encouragement, a helpful introduction for a job seeker, a home-cooked meal for a sick friend. . . . Remember, help and kindness can take many forms.

CHAPTER 8

On "Snowmageddon" and Answered Prayers

Even if you don't live in Atlanta, you may have heard about a rare snowstorm we experienced in the winter of 2014 and the disruptive chaos which followed as the snow turned our roads into sheets of ice when temperatures plummeted into the teens by early evening. Having experienced it firsthand with an eleven-hour commute home, I can assure you real life was much, much worse than what you may have seen on TV or online. This caused dramatic hardship for countless people—from those who left their abandoned cars on the highways to find shelter from the intense cold to the hundreds of children forced to sleep in their schools because they could not get home to their parents. There were a lot of prayers offered up for those most affected by this freakish weather event. Some of these prayers were answered in unusual and profound ways.

It's the subject of "answered prayer" that I want to address in this chapter.

When I left my office that day at noon and joined the thousands of fellow Atlantans trying to get home as the first snowflakes began to fall, I spent the first few hours on the phone with clients or reflecting on business-related issues. My mind was racing over random minutiae until I had to face my first ice-covered hill. I thought of nothing more than getting my car safely over the hill; and by some miracle I did. As I reflected on this close call and tried to calm my rapidly beating heart, I realized that I had fallen into the same trap that has ensnared me so many times in the past. I was attempting to be in control without any help. I was trying to take on the storm, the icy hill, and my dangerous commute home all by myself rather than seek the Lord's help in prayer. I also recognized the recent and reoccurring pattern of being so busy that my prayer life had been getting crowded out by my insane schedule.

If you have read my past work, you know I have frequently referred to asking God for help and receiving exactly what I *needed*, not necessarily what I *wanted*. The storm, in a strange way, provided me with several opportunities to make course corrections in my life. Let me explain.

I desperately needed to be still and listen. The storm forced me to be in a car by myself for almost half a day. When I received the jarring wake-up call on the first icy hill, I felt a surprising sense of peace that had been eluding me during that particular period in my life. I prayed multiple Rosaries in the silence of the car and felt the warm embrace of the Blessed Mother. As I encountered more steep hills and dangerous situations with stranded cars everywhere, I humbly asked God for help and strength. I must have made the Sign of the Cross and blessed myself fifty times that night.

Eight hours into my journey home, I attempted in the darkness to take on a particularly dangerous hill and started slipping backward. I was able to maneuver the car to the side of the road, and I then decided it was time to give in and pull over. At that moment, a stranger appeared out of the snowy darkness and asked me if I could move my car so the large truck in front of me could back up and escape the icy patch where he was stuck. I explained my predicament, and he immediately offered his help in getting me turned around. After a few hair-raising moments, I was on my way again thanks to the kindness of this helpful gentleman.

As I looked for another back road home, I came upon a hotel and decided again that it was too dangerous to continue and would call it a night. Upon entering the lobby, I was surrounded by several dozen people all seeking shelter in this already full hotel. The front desk employees of the hotel confirmed my fears that none of the other hotels in the area had vacancies. Walking back to my car, I reflected on the rejection Joseph and Mary received at the crowded inn. I said yet another prayer and once again attempted to make my way home.

Despite the setback, I retained my peace. I was calm and reflective. I thought a great deal about my wife and sons and how much I loved them. Fond memories of my father's visit for my thirteen-year-old son's birthday a few days before brought a smile to my face. I did an examination of conscience and thought about the sins I needed to confess and looked forward to my next opportunity for Reconciliation.

About two miles from my home, I was forced to detour into a neighboring subdivision because of the icy conditions on the hilly main road. The power was out and there was no light from the homes I passed. I would have been lost if not for the final act of kindness of strangers—neighborhood residents with flashlights were outside guiding the few drivers like me to a route that got us through to a more suitable road. I will never know their names, but I will always be grateful to these good people.

Inching closer to home in the final hour of my snow odyssey, I prayed over and over again for strength and help. I reconnected to what was important during this adventure and felt clearheaded and strangely refreshed after such a harrowing ordeal. I had my priorities straight again and was truly grateful.

I walked through the door of my home almost exactly eleven hours after I left my office into the welcoming embrace of my teary-eyed wife. I was keenly aware at that moment, in addition to the spiritual course correction and epiphanies I received during one of the longest days of my life, that I was blessed to have a wife and sons who loved me. I recognized that I was even more blessed to have a loving Heavenly Father who guided me home.

Have you ever faced an experience like this when you were almost forced to course correct and get back on track? As you reflect on this, what lessons did you learn? How do these lessons show up in your life today? Are you in a tough place now in your life and in need of a significant change?

CHAPTER 9

A God Wink in the Woods

I vividly recall a Saturday afternoon hike earlier this year with Alex at a favorite park near our home. As we trod the familiar walking trail through the woods, I found myself deep in thought about where I should serve next in my parish after having stepped down from leading a ministry there for the last fifteen years. Walking on, my thoughts eventually transitioned to prayer as I turned this dilemma over to God and sought His help. As Alex and I approached the beautiful lake at the center of the park with me still deep in thought, we unexpectedly encountered some familiar faces.

Margaret and Jim, along with a few of their children and grandchildren, greeted us warmly as we approached them. I have known this wonderful couple for several years. Margaret works at my parish and leads the ministry for adults interested in joining the Catholic Church. We exchanged pleasantries, and they asked me how things were going as Alex walked on ahead of me. I shared that I had been praying and discerning a new way to serve the parish and the Church. Their eyes grew large as I shared this, and Jim said that Margaret was actively seeking sponsors to work with those interested in joining the Church. I knew as soon as the words left Jim's mouth that this was where I was being called to serve; there was no doubt in my mind. Margaret asked if I would be interested, and I immediately said yes, promising to follow up that coming Monday.

Why does this seemingly random encounter merit inclusion in this book? I have been going to that park almost every week for more than a decade and had *never* encountered Jim and Margaret there before. At the very moment I finished offering up my prayer for discernment about how and where to serve my parish community, this couple appeared with the perfect opportunity to serve. Coincidence? I think not.

There are many lessons to unpack here, but here are two that clearly stand out for me:

- Don't carry the burden of discernment about important things alone. It is always wise to seek God's help through prayer. He may not always give you the answers you *want*, but He will give you exactly what you *need*.
- Be mindful of the people who may cross your radar or situations that may arise when you are discerning something important. The solution or clues to find the solution may be right in front of your face if you are actively listening, paying attention, and fully present.

I have many stories of God-wink experiences during my frequent walks in these woods. There is something about nature and the quiet of the woods that calms me and heightens my awareness. I have trained myself over the years to be mindful of the people I encounter while hiking and the helpful insights and epiphanies that frequently come to me during these excursions. The effort on my part has been minimal, but the reward has been life-changing.

By the way, the first person I was paired with in the ministry I joined was a wonderful dad in his mid-thirties with two sons. His older son is on the autism spectrum, and the additional blessing of this story is that I had the opportunity to accompany this good man on his faith journey and also offer help and insight from my experience as the father of a child with special needs. God may have called me to serve the Church and my parish through this ministry, but I also know I was *specifically* called to serve this father through our shared experiences. He came into the Catholic Church a few months later as his beautiful family, filled with pride and joy, smiled at him a few pews behind.

When have you discerned something important in your life? How did you do it? Who helped you? What was the outcome? Reflect on the lessons of this story and use them to help you before your next big life or career decision.

CHAPTER 10

A Man I Know

I lit a candle and prayed in our parish chapel not long ago for a man I know in his mid-eighties who is struggling with various health issues as he gets older. The candle I lit burned brightly, more brightly than the others, for the hour I was in the chapel. The light reminded me of this man's life, which was filled with countless good examples and a wonderful legacy of the lives he has touched. Let me tell you a little about him.

He had a challenging childhood. His father left when he was a little boy and he, his two brothers, and his twin sister were raised by his alcoholic mother and grandmother. He made his way through childhood with no real fatherly influence and very little money to keep the household going. He was good at sports and played high school football; he focused on girls and going to the beach as ways to escape the emotional turmoil at home.

He joined the Army at age eighteen, and the military formed the basis for the man he became. He learned self-discipline, gained a work ethic, and became a leader. After six years, he left to join the real world and start his career. He was very different from the rash teenager he had been;

he was now a mature man focused on starting a new life. He met and fell in love with a woman a few years later, and they settled down to start a family.

The happy couple had a boy, and both parents got busy pursuing their careers and raising their child. The man tried college, but after two years decided it was not for him and focused instead on working as hard as he could to support his family. The man created the opposite of his own childhood experience. Although he was not perfect, he always made time after work to play catch with his son and teach him valuable life lessons. He loved talking to his son about the importance of getting a good education, working hard, helping others in need, and always doing your best. This hardworking father grew up in a generation that didn't easily show affection, and he was rarely heard to say, "I love you," but his actions showed the depth of his feelings toward his family more than words ever could.

A daughter was born after the man and his wife moved to Georgia in the early 1970s, and now the family was complete. The years went by, and the man started attending church at the urging of his wife. He found a true calling as a Sunday School teacher and faithful member of his church. The man and woman continued to raise their children. They built a good moral foundation in the home and set great examples with their work ethic and devotion to family. The man was well known in the community as a good friend, hard worker, devout churchgoer, selfless giver, great father, and devoted husband.

He saw first his son off to college, and years later, his daughter. He had always placed a premium on education, and it made him very proud to see his children live out his dream. Disappointments and triumphs followed in the next several years as the man watched his children stumble, fall, and get back up again in their own pursuit of life, love, and happiness. He just kept on working and giving testimony with his life; his children could easily see a great example to follow, even if they didn't always appreciate him.

The later years saw the son raise a family of his own and the daughter get married, have a son, and get divorced. Out of his sense of duty and compassion, he and his wife took their daughter and grandson into their home, and they helped to raise their grandson. The man still taught the timeless lessons of having a good work ethic, strong values, and an education. His happiest moments always seemed to be a teaching opportunity with his daughter's son and the sons of his firstborn.

Today, the man's age, a lifetime of hard work, and a past smoking addiction have caught up with him, and he is dealing with various health challenges. Even when he is not feeling well, though, he always smiles and makes the conversation about you, not him.

I wonder if he recognizes how many lives he has touched by the example of his incredible work ethic, making good moral choices, and always offering to give of himself to others—never asking for anything in return. He was married to the same woman for forty-five years until her death in February 2010, and the dignified and caring way he handled her loss was another grace-filled example to emulate. I hope he knows how he has influenced me by the meaningful life he has led.

The man is known by several names: husband, brother, friend, Papa, and Steve. I have always just called him . . . Dad.

Dad, thank you for being the best example a son could ever want and for showing me how to pursue and live a meaningful life. I hope I pass along what you have taught me to my own children.

What memories of your parents do you cherish most? Have you told them recently how much they mean to you? If not, what is holding you back?

CHAPTER 11

The Tour Guide's Quick-Thinking and a Lesson in Patience at the Duomo

My wife and I were fortunate in May 2023 to take our family to Italy for vacation after our younger son graduated from college. We visited Rome, Florence, the Tuscany towns of Siena and San Gimignano, and Lake Como during our eleven-day visit. It was an amazing trip, filled with incredible sights, experiences, and memories we will cherish forever.

As you may be aware, one of the largest and most beautiful churches in the world is the Duomo, or Florence Cathedral of Santa Maria del Fiore. Any trip to Florence must include a visit inside this beautiful Gothic-style church and the famous dome designed by Filippo Brunelleschi; it is a proud symbol of the city and the Renaissance period in history. We had marked the Duomo as one of our primary sights of interest from the beginning of our trip planning and looked forward to going inside this amazing church that, until our visit, had only existed in our imaginations and through online pictures.

I will never forget the third day of our four-day stay in Florence. We were guided by a wonderful private tour guide named Patrizia. She was a native Florentine, a professor at a local university, and worked as a tour guide part-time. She was full of fun and very knowledgeable, and she gave our family expert guidance as we toured the city and museums she knew so well. One of the last stops on our itinerary that day was the Opera del Duomo Museum, which contained beautiful works of art by the famous artists who contributed to the Duomo and other historical artifacts associated with this famous church. As our copy of the itinerary from the travel agency clearly stated, our museum tour was to be followed by the long-anticipated visit inside the Duomo.

I was cranky and tired, as were the rest of my family, at the end of that long day. We were impatient to visit the Duomo, especially as we were rapidly approaching 6:00 p.m. when we knew the church tours ended. This was our only chance to visit the Duomo since we would be in the Tuscan countryside all the next day. I asked Patrizia at 5:30 p.m. when we could head across the square to the Duomo for the last stop on our tour. She looked puzzled and said her instructions from the agency were to only guide us through the Opera del Duomo museum and not the Duomo itself.

I am usually a fairly calm person, but Patrizia could clearly see my frustration, and she could tell that my family and I were disappointed. We were all tired, ready to give in, call it a day, and carry the regret of this missed opportunity with us. She asked us to give her a few minutes as she called the travel agency, speaking heatedly in Italian with them for several minutes. Patrizia ended her call, looked at us thoughtfully for a minute, and said, "Here is what we are going to do. You have shared with me that you are Catholic, and I am also Catholic. Because I live in Florence, I happen to know there is a special Mass at 6:00 p.m. today inside the Duomo for the Solemnity of Saints Zenobius and Antoninus, two of Florence's most celebrated bishops. Anyone can attend, but only locals will know about it. Come with me—we are going to that Mass!"

We immediately agreed and our disappointment gave way to genuine excitement as we scurried across the square to a side door where a few people were walking in for Mass. We entered one of the most beautiful churches I have ever seen. It was truly breathtaking. Patrizia led us to a side altar where Mass was being celebrated by a few priests with a number of senior Church officials in attendance. There may have been a total of thirty people present, including our family.

After this solemn and beautiful Mass, celebrated in both Italian and Latin, Patrizia said we were free to look around and take pictures if we wished. We experienced the beauty, art, and history of this world-famous church in relative silence because of the small number of people present. The beautiful mural painted inside the top of the dome alone was worth the visit. The Duomo visit and the chance to celebrate this special Mass was one of our favorite experiences, and we were so grateful for Patrizia's kindness, calmness under pressure, and quick thinking for making it happen. We thanked her profusely before parting ways that evening, and we count our experience with this thoughtful guide and genuinely good person as a highlight of our Italian adventure.

Was this a God wink moment? A lesson about the virtue of patience? I only know that Patrizia saved the day and allowed me and my loved ones to share in a profound experience we will never forget. Sometimes we simply have to be patient and calmly endure frustration and obstacles, trusting that something good awaits us on the other side. Sometimes, if we are paying attention, we will be more aware of good people all around us waiting to offer help or perhaps guide us to a better place in life.

Reflect on a time when you faced adversity and almost gave up but endured a little longer to experience a positive outcome. Have you ever placed your faith in a friend, family member, work colleague or total stranger to help you deal with a difficult situation? How might you look for opportunities to be a Patrizia to someone else and help them overcome adversity or obstacles in their life?

CHAPTER 12

A Public Witness

Saying a blessing and making the Sign of the Cross before a meal in a restaurant may not seem like a big deal to you. Or perhaps it feels like the opposite—a significant public profession of faith that makes you uncomfortable.

I am reminded of a lunch I had several years ago with a new client. Our working partnership had been very business-focused since the beginning, and I wanted to forge the stronger personal connection that I enjoy with most of my clients. We made small talk about a number of subjects until our food arrived. I offered to say a blessing over our meal and told her she was welcome to join me. As I made the Sign of the Cross and started to pray, I noticed that she also made the Sign of the Cross. I smiled to myself and said an additional internal prayer of thanks for the opportunity I had been given.

Between bites of salad, I asked her which parish she attended. She gave me a funny look before responding with the parish name, then added, "That's a long story." I told her I would love to hear about it. For the next half hour, we talked about her faith journey, her family, how much she loved her parish, her devotion to the Blessed Mother, and her prayer life. The stale, business-focused exchange at the beginning of the meal had been replaced by a warm conversation about our shared faith. I certainly achieved my goal of a stronger personal connection!

As we were preparing to leave our table, she shared that she never spoke of her faith in business settings and had really enjoyed our discussion. As we were walking out of the restaurant, we speculated on why Catholics don't seem to discuss faith as openly as our Protestant brethren do. I suggested it may be fear of judgment or lack of confidence in explaining the teachings of the Church. She suggested that it all came down to simple courage.

I asked her to explain. She pointed out, "When you made the Sign of the Cross in a crowded restaurant and said the blessing out loud, I realized that I never do that. My fear of saying a simple blessing is a clear reminder to me that I don't often have the courage to share my faith outside of my comfort zone. I am grateful you don't have that issue and also for this wonderful conversation."

Driving back to my office, I reflected on countless other business meals over the years that had turned into faith and other personal discussions, perhaps because of the simple act of making the Sign of the Cross and blessing the meal. I don't know if I see this as courageous as much as trying to be authentic and following the call of Christ. It's certainly food for thought and worthy of careful reflection.

What would happen if everyone who reads this makes a simple commitment to say a blessing (consistent with their faith tradition) over every meal from now on, regardless of their companions? How many incredible discussions would occur as a result of this simple and public act of faith?

Yes, one could easily argue the other side and share the possible negative outcomes. But all the encouragement we need can be found in the words of Jesus:

"Everyone who acknowledges me before others I will acknowledge before my heavenly Father. But whoever denies me before others, I will deny before my heavenly Father." (Matthew 10:32-33)

Does this story affirm your own practice of saying a blessing over meals, regardless of your companions? Does it challenge you to consider embracing the practice for all the reasons I shared?

CHAPTER 13

The Hectic Pace of Life

In addition to my regular daily prayer routine, I long ago committed to praying an hour each week in the small chapel within my parish. This hour each week of reflection and prayer has been the inspiration for much of my writing and the catalyst for countless other blessings in my life.

I vividly remember going to my prayer hour one morning several years ago with a sincere desire to simply be still and listen. I habitually struggle with too much "noise" in my life, and I wanted to offer up my burdens in prayer, ask for help, and patiently wait for quiet and peace to take over.

My mind was calm and peaceful for only a few minutes before the usual cacophony of annoying voices in my head began to sound off. *Why hasn't Jesus answered me yet? I wonder if my 9:00 a.m. meeting will go well . . . I have a million emails to answer . . . I wonder what's for dinner.*

I was in the chapel for five minutes, and I was already in trouble!

Rather than give in to frustration, I decided to think about my actions and examine where I was falling short. I prayed for guidance as I replayed the events of the previous months in my mind. What I realized as I recalled the highly caffeinated and frantic pace I had been keeping was that I was engaging in the workaholic behaviors I thought I had rid myself of many years ago when I came into the Church with my family. Instead of enjoying the quiet prayer and reflection I so dearly love early each morning, I was filling that time with social media, answering emails, and other work-related activity.

The daily examen that provided me brief moments of prayer and reflection throughout my busy day had been crowded out by meetings, calls, and other excuses. My laptop had been getting pulled out after dinner too frequently, which negatively impacted family time and opportunities for my wife and I to enjoy some quiet moments together. I felt like I was racing toward a cliff—and I needed a course correction!

Since quiet prayer was not working and reflecting on my recent hectic schedule left me feeling deflated, I decided to focus on my spiritual reading to look for inspiration and help. I have found great comfort and wisdom over the years in the writings of Fr. Francis Fernandez and his wonderful series of books *In Conversation with God*. I turned to the meditation for that day in Volume 3, which is on the dignity of work. The light bulb went off for me a few minutes later as I read the passage I so desperately needed:

Work should not take up so much of our day that it occupies the time that should be dedicated to God, to the family, to our friends. . . . If this should happen it would be a clear sign that we are not sanctifying ourselves through our work, but rather we are simply seeking self-satisfaction in it.[1]

I had allowed myself to believe that all of the hard work in my professional life and non-profit service was always for others, when perhaps one of my motivations had been for my own self-satisfaction. It was hard to admit, but I think there was some truth to it.

I circled back in my mind to how I had begun my hour of prayer when I asked the Lord for help. From the gift of self-awareness He gave me in reflecting on my recent behaviors and the realization I needed to make some big changes to the revelation He showed me in the writings of Fr. Fernandez, Jesus absolutely answered my prayer that day. He gave me all that I asked for . . . and everything He knew I needed. After that hour, I knew I would have some hard work and a lot of prayer ahead of me to make the necessary changes I needed to restore peace and a sense of balance.

Noise, distractions, and losing sight of what is truly important is a common problem for many of us, and I fully recognize that I will be addressing this issue for the rest of my life. It's difficult in today's world to find peace, and when my overactive brain won't not allow me to be calm, the experience rattles me. I knew I needed to adjust my behavior, but I wasn't quite sure how to begin.

The weeks following this experience were a combination of maintaining my typical fast pace, snatches of inconsistent prayer time, and infrequent reflection on how I had gotten so

1 Fr. Francis Fernandez, *In Conversation with God, Volume 3* (Strongsville, OH: Scepter Publishers, 1989), 259.

far off course. Then I got sick with pneumonia. I had to cancel my meeting schedule for almost two weeks and was forced to work from home as I regained my health. In retrospect, I now recognize the hand of God in my forced "retreat," and this was an additional warning to slow down a bit.

My crazy schedule had been forcibly addressed and a few valuable lessons had been learned about not ignoring my health, but I was still struggling with the noise issue as we were approaching Ash Wednesday. I had still not decided what I would give up for Lent when I joined my family for Mass that evening and heard a riveting homily from our parochial vicar, Father Henry. He talked about removing the obstacles between us and Christ during Lent. He challenged us to examine what was getting in the way of a stronger relationship with Him and to give up those things during Lent.

Listening to him, I realized I desperately needed more quiet time. I would never have peace and a return to the rich prayer life I once enjoyed unless I eliminated my distractions. So, I gave up radio, TV, and unnecessary computer time during that Lent, and I have minimized these distractions as much as possible since then. This change has had an enormous impact on my life.

Before you decide that I'm nuts and this is not doable, indulge me for a little longer. I don't open my laptop in the morning until I have prayed, done some reading or creative writing, and had breakfast. When I am in my car, I often turn the radio off and enjoy the silence. I have significantly limited TV time and have replaced it with more reading time, board games with my family, or reading together as a family. I punctuate my days with windows of exercise and walking when

I can, often praying when I walk. All of this is helping me more fully honor my priorities of God, family, and work and bring more peace and calm into my life. I wish I had realized sooner the incredible difference all these changes would make!

What have I learned from these experiences? All my hard work is meaningless if it is not given up for God's greater glory instead of my own personal satisfaction. I have learned that I'm not Superman and need to be careful about overscheduling my life.

The commotion and hectic pace of the lives we lead may always be an issue, but we can modify our behaviors, eliminate some distractions, and be more intentional about how we spend our time. I know I was made for heaven and not this place. I may always be stumbling toward peace and my final destination, but at least I am on the right path and moving forward—and that is a good place to start.

How are you dealing with the noise and busyness of your life? What have you done to address it? What can you eliminate or replace with a better alternative in your daily life that will help you achieve the peace and calm you may be craving?

CHAPTER 14

The Difference an Hour Can Make

At the end of 2014, on the Monday between Christmas and New Year's Day, I had to work for part of the day. I met a few clients, tied up loose ends for the year, and did some preparation for the New Year. It was challenging to be pulled away from my family over the holidays, especially with my easily bored sons out of school during the break. I felt guilty, but I also needed to be a good steward of my business and financial responsibilities.

The last meeting of the day was to be a late lunch with a new client prospect that had been scheduled several weeks before. He called me thirty minutes before our appointment to apologize and say he couldn't make it. We rescheduled our meeting for another day, and suppressing mild irritation, I found myself with an unexpected extra hour.

What to do? Well, I had a pile of paperwork back at my office to be handled. Perhaps I could leave messages for some of my clients or send them emails in an effort to start filling up my meeting calendar after the holidays. Maybe I could find a quiet place and write that new business blog post that had been on my mind for weeks.

I did none of these things and went home instead.

Maybe it was guilt or the prompting of the Holy Spirit, but nothing at that very moment seemed as important as going home to my wife and sons. As I pulled into the driveway, I saw my thirteen-year-old son, Ryan, practicing his jump shot with the new basketball he received for Christmas. Without any words being exchanged, we took turns shooting baskets for half an hour. We were simply a father and son having fun together and enjoying being with each other.

Then he broke the silence. "Dad, can we talk about why that kid committed suicide?"

My son's jarring question was referring to a local high school student who had killed himself three weeks before, which our family had discussed over dinner one night right after the tragedy.

After talking about the possible reasons why this young man had chosen to end his own life, we talked about how difficult it is for kids today to deal with the enormous pressure schools, peers, society, and even their own families place on them. I think my son was relieved to talk about this topic (he said it had been on his mind for days), and he seemed reassured after we finished. I was very grateful at that moment to be reassured that my son takes his faith seriously and understands the wonderful recourse we have to prayer when we face difficulties. I am especially glad he felt comfortable talking to me about this painful subject rather than tackling it on his own.

Maybe only other fathers will understand, but I was even more grateful to be there for my son at that moment when he needed to get something off his chest and hear guidance and an explanation from someone he trusted. I would have missed this wonderful opportunity if I had opted for one of the various noncritical tasks I could have chosen instead. There is a profound lesson here that really hit home for me: *We need to be more mindful of the choices we make about where we spend our time, especially if we are choosing between work and our loved ones.*

As we consider where we spend our time, I encourage all of us to put more thinking and discernment into our busy schedules and recognize that we may need to reset our priorities. Are we letting the unimportant crowd out the important? Are we missing opportunities like the one I was blessed to have with my son because of paperwork, catching up on emails, or returning one more phone call? Do we control our calendars or do our calendars control us? Do we have a disproportionate focus on the pursuit of worldly things when we could be spending more time in prayer, with our loved ones, or in the service of others in need?

In that conversation with my son, I witnessed for myself the incredible difference an hour can make. As we look ahead, what difference will our choices about how we spend our time have on what matters most in life? Remember that one of the most meaningful gifts we can give our families and friends doesn't require fancy wrapping and a big red bow. This gift is simply called *time.*

Can you find an extra hour this week to spend with someone you love? How can you be more discerning about the choice between nonessential work and meaningful time with the people you care about most?

CHAPTER 15

The Value of Struggle

One of the defining moments in my youngest son's life occurred on a Saturday years ago when he was nine years old. He had been working hard for over two years to earn his black belt in Tae Kwon Do and was participating in an all-city testing event to determine if he was ready. He executed his kicks and moves flawlessly during the day, and we could feel the tension and excitement growing as the kids approached the final test: breaking a board with a flying kick.

The students had two chances to break the board, and my son's first kick failed. There was enormous pressure on him at the end of this long day to break the board or he would not earn his black belt and would have to wait another four months to be retested. His turn came and with a determined look in his eyes, he began to run toward the instructors who were holding the board in their hands. He leaped into the air, cocked his leg, and lashed out with his foot at the board. The whole scene seemed to unfold in slow motion as we watched the board bend slightly but not break. He had mistimed the kick, and his second chance to break the board failed—he would not be leaving with the coveted black belt that day. As it turned out, the other six kids in his age group also failed to break the board. We wondered how our son would react to this disappointment.

We walked over and hugged him, noticing the other upset children in his group being consoled by their parents. To our great surprise, Ryan was stoic about the whole thing: "That's OK; I'll just practice harder and take the test again." We were blown away by his response and complimented him for being so mature about what had happened.

To bring Ryan's part of the story to conclusion, he worked hard over the next four months, broke the board at the next testing, and finally earned his black belt. It meant a great deal to him, especially since he failed in his first attempt. That black belt represented in his young mind something he wanted and worked very hard to earn. His failed first attempt was simply an obstacle he had to overcome.

Imagine what would have happened if the officials running that first testing had said, "You all tried really hard, and you each deserve to get a black belt today." What lessons would our son have learned if he had been given a reward that he did not earn? Does the real (adult) world give awards for trying hard?

My oldest son, Alex, is one of my role models and a true inspiration as I watch him navigate through each day with his challenges. I can never complain about anything when I consider what he goes through in his life. When he was thirteen, our son wanted to earn what is called Level R at his school. This is the recognition that he is demonstrating leadership qualities, and it comes with special privileges—including lunch off campus once a week. The students and teachers meet once a week in a "community meeting" to discuss and vote on who goes up or down in the school's level system.

Three times Alex tried to move up but was voted down each time because of some areas he needed to improve. We were getting anxious as we observed this happening, but we knew we needed to let it run its course. On the fourth attempt, he finally made it to Level R. His beaming face and the excitement he felt about this achievement was very moving. He worked very hard to stay at that level all year, and the hard work spilled over into strong academic performance and a slew of awards he received on Honor's Day at the end of the year.

What would have happened if the school had felt sorry for him and just let him move up the first time? What if we had intervened and not allowed him to keep trying for Level R? The positive impact of this struggle made a huge difference in his success that year for which my wife and I are very grateful.

In speaking with parents over the years and observing my own children's sports and school activities, I have noticed a disturbing trend: There is a powerful reluctance to let our kids struggle or fail. We are not raising resilient children. Fairness is the new mantra. We worry more about our children's self-esteem than preparing them for an independent and successful future. Everyone gets a nice trophy or certificate for simply showing up. Competition is often set aside in favor of participation where everybody is a winner.

Don't get me wrong—I like fairness. I'm also strongly in favor of encouraging young people. But I also appreciate the pursuit of excellence. Competition can be a healthy thing that also encourages children to excel and give their best effort on the playing field and in school. Instead of assuming that our kids might be hurt or negatively impacted by failure or struggle, perhaps we should consider that they will learn valuable lessons from these experiences. I think we know intuitively as parents that we are molded by our childhood experiences. How were you shaped by your childhood? How does your upbringing manifest itself in how you are raising your family today? How does it affect your actions at work? How does it affect your faith? Can you trace your actions as an adult to the multitude of experiences you had as a child? Children need to learn from their struggles and failures and experience the accompanying emotions of sadness and frustration. These struggles will teach them to be persistent in the face of adversity later in life and help them build resilience.

If we fix every problem and swoop in at the first sign of struggle, will our children be able to deal with challenges as adults? Statistics indicate that kids are living with their parents much longer than they did thirty years ago. Many are moving back home after they finish college. Generational expert and author Dr. Tim Elmore, president of Growing Leaders, is fond of saying that "twenty-six is the new eighteen." Young people, often unequipped by their parents, coaches, and teachers to deal with the harsh realities of life, are staying home longer under the protective umbrella of their parents. How do we make the necessary changes to equip our kids to be independent, confident, resilient, and successful in life?

Six Best Practices to Consider

Perhaps the first step in solving the problem is to honestly admit that we might have one. We can blame others, but ultimately the responsibility for raising our kids and preparing them for the future belongs to us. I have come up with six best practices from my family's experiences (and ongoing struggles) along with observations of other families for your consideration:

1. ***Be a parent, not a friend.*** My wife and I have raised our kids to hopefully love and respect us, not think of us as friends. We can be friends when they are thirty and have families of their own. Unlike friends, parents have to give tough love, provide boundaries, and equip kids to face the world outside of the home. There will be lots of laughter and tears on this kind of journey.

2. ***Teach the value of money.*** My parents did three things for me that had a positive and powerful impact on my life: 1) They gave me a used lawnmower when I was ten so I could start a lawn business and make my own money; 2) they told me I would have to save up to buy my own car; and 3) they let me know from my early teens that they could contribute very little to my college expenses and I would need to save, work during school, and take out loans, which I did. It was a struggle during those years, but I gained an appreciation for hard work and the value of a dollar that I am grateful for today. What's the lesson?

Don't provide everything for your children. Make them earn it and they will appreciate it more.

3. ***Everything your kids do is* not *amazing!*** If we praise everything our kids do, even poor or mediocre performance, how will they gain perspective or achieve excellence? Encourage them to do their best, show them how to get better, and teach them to practice. If they get a C on a test, have them correct the items they missed. If they are struggling on the athletic field, speak to the coach so they can get in some extra practice. Show them excellence and how to achieve it. Don't sugarcoat mediocre efforts or you might cripple them for life.

4. ***Don't keep your kids in an ivory tower.*** Use discretion as to the right age for this but talk to your kids about the real world (they are likely getting inundated with mixed messages and information online already). Kids are smarter and wiser than we sometimes give them credit for and they can readily absorb important lessons. Talk about the realities of living within a family budget. Discuss how much it costs to attend college these days. Discuss your job and career journey, current events, global problems, politics, etc. Treating kids like responsible members of the family will prepare them to better handle the challenges of being adults in society.

5. ***Teach selfless giving at a young age.*** If you want your kids to appreciate what they have in life, get them involved in nonprofit volunteering and community service as soon as they are able. Serving at a soup kitchen, building houses, picking up trash, or simply spending time with senior citizens at a retirement home will help

them gain a better appreciation for the life you have provided them and plant a lesson about the blessings received by giving selflessly to others.

6. ***Be a family of faith.*** I have often written about the necessity of parents being strong role models for children. My wife and I have a responsibility to teach our kids to love God and understand grow in faith. We have taught them to pray. They will be most likely to do these things if we set the right example. Equipping our kids with a strong faith will exponentially increase their ability to deal with adversity in the future when they know they are not alone and Christ is always with them. Looking for a teaching moment? Let your children see you on your knees every night in prayer and faithfully attend church together every week.

Our natural parenting instincts are always going to kick in when our kids face struggles or roadblocks. For their sake, especially as they get into school and start playing sports, let's exercise restraint in protecting them from failure. In our conversations with teachers and coaches, let's be attuned to their styles and look for opportunities to influence them to challenge our kids more. Perhaps we should seek more challenging school and sport alternatives if necessary. If we want our kids to cope successfully with an often unfriendly and challenging world, we need to teach them these lessons in their early years. The world, especially the business world, is a tough place. It is not going to nurture, coddle, or protect our children when they are old enough to have real jobs and there will certainly not be awards handed out for participation.

If we truly love our children, can we love them enough to let them learn valuable lessons from their struggles? For their sake, I hope so.

How have your past struggles, especially when you were living at home with your parents or caregivers, shaped you into the person you are today? What were the key lessons you learned? How are you passing these lessons on to your own children or the young people you coach or mentor at work or in your personal life?

CHAPTER 16

The Joys and Challenges of Modern Fatherhood

Sometimes I can almost imagine myself as a great father to my children . . . and then I do something to mess it up. I vividly recall a past October many years ago when my boys and I welcomed my wife home from a five-day trip to California where she had been visiting her sister. What started out as my great adventure with the kids at the beginning of her trip turned into exhaustion at the end, and I guiltily looked forward to my wife's coming home so I could escape to my work and other activities. I had just experienced a great time with my sons (we really *did* have fun), and now I was looking to flee the scene and get back to activities that weren't nearly as important. *What was my problem?*

I wanted to provide my sons with the parental role model they deserved. My desire has always been for them to grow up to be good men and great fathers, and I knew that every moment I spent with them was a learning opportunity. Yet as those five days came to an end, because of the enormous demands on my time during the day, I was looking forward to getting a break, and this placed a significant burden of guilt on my heart.

After my wife returned from that week away, I carried these thoughts into the weekend and did a lot of praying. I asked God for help and a path to follow that would help me step up to my responsibilities. I asked Him for the peace and courage to deal with being a better father in these challenging times. I wondered if I needed to see some role models or examples to help me get closer to the better father I wanted to be.

Sometimes God answers prayer very promptly and clearly.

After that weekend of prayer and reflection, I received four powerful reminders of the real meaning of fatherhood in the days that followed. The hand of God was clearly at work, and all of what happened next is still burned in my brain. I will never forget the impact it had on me.

The following Tuesday afternoon, I was driving back from a doctor visit with my oldest son when I decided to call my father in Florida. We exchanged idle chitchat for a few minutes, and then I shared my recent fatherhood dilemma with him. He listened silently. When I finished, he offered this sage observation: "Randy, I think you need to give yourself a break. I was never a perfect father, and I made my share of mistakes, but I always knew God would find a way to help me and make up for my shortcomings. I also think one of the best things I did for you and your sister was to make sure you knew how much I loved your mom."

I reflected on the conversation with my father as we walked into Mass for All Saints Day later that week: *not perfect . . . God will help me . . . love my wife.* I began thinking of St. Joseph and his amazing example as a husband and a father. He was a good and simple man who trusted God, took the pregnant Mary as his wife, and raised Jesus as his own son. I have always found peace by asking St. Joseph for his intercession, and I did so again on that All Saints Day. In my own father and in the patron saint of fathers, I had rediscovered my role models.

The next day was a bit traumatic for my family, as Alex was to have a tube placed in his left ear for the eighth time. He was very anxious about the operation as we drove to the outpatient surgery center. All went well, and I was relieved to see him as they rolled his bed into the room where I was waiting. I looked down on my firstborn and stroked his hair, finding it hard to believe he was now a teenager. The outpouring of love I felt at that moment for my son and his younger brother reminded me of the incredible joys of being a father and of what is important in life. God created these children and gave them to my wife and me. We are truly blessed to be their parents.

After getting my son home for my wife to take care of him, I returned to a pile of work at the office and plowed through it as fast as possible so I could get home and see how he was doing. As I walked in the door, feeling tired, distracted, and a little guilty (again), my younger son ran up to me with a poster he had made in school. He said, "Dad, what do you think of my poster? Take a look at the bottom on the left. Do you like it?" The section was called "My Dad," and he described me this way:

He spends a lot of time with me and tells me things.
He plays sports with me and takes me to lacrosse practice.
We pray together.
He started writing books a few years ago,
and I am very proud of him.
I want to write like him some day.
I love my dad.

After wiping away a few tears, it dawned on me that if we ever want to get a report card on how we are doing, maybe we should ask our children.

Have you or someone you love been through the same kinds of struggles I have experienced? These struggles have taught me that I can't carry the burden of being a father by myself. I need to be humble and ask for help. I will more frequently seek out the sage advice of my father, the intercession of St. Joseph, the support of other great dads I know, and most importantly, the help of our Heavenly Father in prayer. I will make sure my kids know how much I love their mother. If I do these things faithfully, I trust I will more fully experience the blessings and joys of being a father to these wonderful boys.

Have you ever felt like you were failing as a parent? How did you get back on track? Where do you turn for help and inspiration?

CHAPTER 17

Hidden Blessings

It is difficult to be a parent today, especially if you have a child with special needs. The days are emotional roller coaster rides often filled with frustration and only fleeting glimpses of progress. These families often push the pause button on their old lives as the focus becomes all about therapists, adaptive learning, fighting with schools for support, medication regimens, special diets, etc., etc. The expenses are astronomical and sacrifices are made that other families would never understand. Each day is a battle for survival, which requires fully engaged mothers, fathers, and often siblings to pitch in and make things work. This effort can be physically exhausting. The emotional toll on the parents and "typical" children in this kind of family can be dramatic and is often overlooked in the pursuit of mere survival. The social isolation that often occurs almost becomes a blessing as the family grows weary of explaining about their child to friends and neighbors. It's easier to retreat in an unhealthy way into the safe cocoon of their homes where the uncomfortable looks and questions can't reach them.

But these children are also a great blessing and a gift from God if the choice is made to see them in this light. Once the family finally learns to measure progress in different ways, it's cause for celebration when a positive report comes from school or a new plateau is conquered with the physical therapist. Sometimes, encouraging comments from the speech therapist about new words being pronounced correctly or an improvement in a social exchange feed the parents morsels of hope that maybe, someday, their child will be able to function in a world that often appears frustrating, alien, and even hostile to them. When the family learns to accept this unique gift from God and stops hoping and praying for a more perfect version of what God gave them, hearts are permanently changed, and love flows more freely.

I know all of this because I have an insider's viewpoint. There are days when Alex, now twenty-six, will ask us dozens of questions about our favorite movies, favorite restaurants, discuss upcoming Peloton workouts he wants to do, or try to entice us into several rounds of his favorite board games. Our daily focus on helping him to lead an independent life and take care of himself doesn't always go as we hoped, and we sometimes fear for the worst when we will no longer be around to take care of him.

How do we cope? My wife and I pray a lot. We pray for acceptance. We pray for patience and peace. We pray to be stronger parents and ask the Lord to help us with burdens that seem too great at times. We pray for our son's future and the future of our younger son. We support and love each other and work hard at having a good marriage and honoring our vocation as parents. We remember to be thankful for the great part-time job Alex has and the wonderful people at our church who have embraced him, loved him, and helped him find ways to be a part of parish life. We remind ourselves that God is a loving Father who has great plans for our son that we may not yet fully understand.

As I was thinking about my approach to writing this chapter, I remembered the first day of Advent 2016. Our oldest son enjoys Advent and Christmas. He understands that Jesus is coming into the world, and he wants to be ready. He loves gift giving and that year spent his own money on a present for my wife that he helped me wrap and place under our tree. My wife and I, along with our younger son, listened to Christmas music as we decorated our tree, while Alex stood apart, listening to his own music as usual. That was OK. He just liked the moment and being with the rest of the family. Later that evening after dinner, he was bursting with excitement as he said a blessing over our Advent wreath and read, as part of our family tradition, the Gospel passage for the First Week of Advent.

That night as we finished our family prayers and he crawled into bed, he smiled at me and said, "I love Advent and Christmas. This is my favorite time of the year."

My son may struggle with autism, but in that moment, all I saw was a child who has blessed my life in countless ways and given me much more than I have ever given him. When he smiled at me, he looked like an angel sent from Heaven—an angel sent to remind me that Jesus is coming and I must be ready with a joy-filled heart like that of my son.

Thank you, my dear son, for teaching me another powerful lesson. Thank you, Heavenly Father, for the gift of this child and for choosing me to be his dad.

Do you have a child with special challenges? How do you cope? Or maybe you know someone who has a child with special needs. For your benefit, or maybe for the benefit of someone else, remember the hidden blessings that come from all children, regardless of their challenges.

CHAPTER 18

A Life-Changing Pivot

I vividly recall a summer several years ago when I recognized that I had once again gotten offtrack with my priorities. I had just returned home after my fourth out-of-state speaking trip in six weeks to promote my latest book. I was grateful for the opportunities to speak all over the country, meet new people, and sell books, but I was having serious doubts about whether this was the best use of my time. Every trip I took was valuable time away from my family, and I felt I was in danger of slipping back into the misplaced priorities and bad habits I had abandoned at the beginning of 2000 and described in chapter five.

Around this time, my wonderful wife lovingly but firmly asked me to prayerfully consider if I had my priorities in order. My wife is very insightful, smart, and often sees things I miss. Her thoughtful challenge and my own existing misgivings forced me to carefully evaluate every aspect of my life. *What was my calling? What was my mission and purpose? How did I get offtrack?* I have always been drawn to the idea of serving and helping others, but perhaps I was going about it the wrong way.

After weeks of prayer and reflection, it finally dawned on me that I was guilty of making big decisions about my life and *then* asking God to validate them. Traveling all over the country seemed like a good idea, and I truly believed I was helping others, but if I am honest, I did it because I wanted to do it and not because I felt God was asking this of me. I strive to make my priorities God, family, and work . . . in that order . . . and I had been foolishly placing my work—and maybe even my own ego—at the top of the priority list.

I went through a cathartic period in the months that followed as I reconsidered how I ran my business, promoted my work, and most importantly, how I spent time on my faith, family, health, and friendships. After a lot of prayer and discernment, it struck me that my greatest opportunity to serve and help others was through the individual encounters I am fortunate to have with the large network in the Southeast I have built over the years.

In my professional life, I began to put my full focus on making a positive impact in the lives of the coaching and leadership consulting clients I am fortunate to work with each day as well as anyone else who crosses my path. Being fully present, asking the right questions and actively listening to each person with a sincere desire to serve is where I am at my best . . . and most likely able to truly help others. I still travel on occasion and I have many global clients, but it is much less frequent with the growth of virtual meeting tools, and I try to take my family with me if travel cannot be avoided. The main focus is thinking, acting, serving *locally*.

In my personal life, the significant pivot in my professional life has ensured that the practice of my faith, time with my family, focus on my health, and time with my friends receives the appropriate higher prioritization they deserve. This plays out in my deepening prayer life, my healthy marriage, strong relationships with my children, the focus on my health, and quality time spent with friends and serving the community. By focusing on these important areas *before* my work, my professional life has thrived and my clients consistently see me at my best and receive the highest quality work I can deliver.

As I have pondered the course correction I made over a decade ago (and still work on every day), I am grateful for both my wife's willingness to challenge me and the pivot I was able to make in my life. I am grateful for the virtue of humility as I recognized that my ego was getting in the way. I am appreciative of the sense of peace and joy I feel that only comes from having my priorities in the right place and helping others. I strive every day through my coaching, consulting, books, marriage, parenting, friendships and nonprofit work to influence positive outcomes for the people I encounter in my life. I make a lot of mistakes and certainly don't have all the answers, but I am once again clear about my priorities and how I will spend my time in the service of others. The path to get here had many twists and turns, but I have attempted to be very intentional along the way, and I'm grateful for the countless lessons I've learned.

Reflect for a few minutes on your own life. Are your priorities in order? Have you made a similar course correction or pivot to get back on track? If not, what might need to change?

CHAPTER 19

Gifts

I have been incredibly fortunate over the course of my time on this earth to receive invaluable gifts that have made a tremendous difference in every aspect of my life. I'm not talking about new cars, a new watch, or a new shirt for Christmas. I'm referring to the thoughtful gifts from family, friends, and even relative strangers that have changed my thinking, inspired me, taught me valuable lessons, and gotten me back on track when I was lost.

Let me share a few that really stand out in my memory:

- **Gifts of wisdom** . . . from my parents when I was younger that were often subtle and exactly what I needed at the time, even though I was often resistant and unwilling to listen. This wisdom has echoed through the generations as I find myself sharing my parents' lessons with my own children.
- **The gift of inspiration** . . . from my oldest son, Alex. His joyful willingness to engage with a world each day that is often hostile and alien to people with special needs inspires me and everyone who knows him.

- **The gift of understanding the need to allow others to help me** . . . from my good friend Jim who cared enough about me over a decade ago to help me understand that although I enjoyed helping others, I struggled to let others help me. His helpful advice was a game-changer as I began to work on receiving the help I so enjoy giving to others.
- **The gift of doing work I love** . . . from so many friends who encouraged me to start my own company in 2013. Their willingness to push me out of my comfort zone of low risk tolerance to do work I am passionate about as a solo entrepreneur was the spark that gave me the courage to launch Serviam Partners.
- **The gift of self-reflection** . . . that began to grow as I recognized—with my wife's help— the need to slow down the hectic place of my life over a decade ago and be more fully present for my loved ones, friends, and causes I care about. Being able to pause and reflect on lessons learned and special moments has been an invaluable gift.

I could name dozens of other gifts that have had a meaningful impact on my life. If we slow down enough to appreciate and be present in the encounters we have with others each day, we will begin to see the endless stream of gifts we may be receiving and the difference these gifts are making in our lives. Once we develop this self-awareness about the value and power of what we may be receiving from others, we can more intentionally share our own gifts—such as candid advice for a co-worker, sharing a helpful book, lending a listening ear for a troubled friend, coaching a younger colleague, sharing a little hard-fought wisdom with our children, and more. Mastering the concept of gifts I have shared here will make your life and the lives of everyone around you richer and more rewarding.

Reflect on the memorable and life-changing gifts you have received from others like the ones I describe in this chapter. Reach out and thank the givers.

Consider how you can pass along your own gifts in a more intentional way through the daily interactions you will have with others, enriching both your own life and theirs in the process.

CHAPTER 20

Choosing Between Grumpy and Grateful

I was reflecting recently on the times in which we live. With another nasty political season in full swing, a challenging economy, the eroding of important values in our society, the lack of civility, and a host of other challenges, I could rightfully be in a grumpy state of mind. It also dawned on me that I have a clear choice—a choice between feeling *grumpy* or feeling *grateful*.

I am choosing to feel *grateful*.

I am grateful for many things. These last few years, while difficult, have brought my family closer together. We have become more resilient, and we have been able to take several memorable trips together—trips we have dreamed of for several years. We have all worked on our physical health, and our prayer lives have never been stronger. My businesses are thriving, and I am grateful to do work that I love with amazing clients. I have friends I cherish, and I'm grateful to have them in my life. My faith life is flourishing.

If we take the time to reflect on the good things and blessings in our lives, we will likely find ample reasons to be grateful. Gratitude is always a healthy substitute for frustration, envy, anger, and a host of other negative emotions.

Currently, I am working on three practical actions each day to help me maintain a grateful mindset:

- *Three things I am grateful for.* I don't go to sleep without saying a prayer of thanks for at least three things I am grateful for in my life. This seems simple, but it is a powerful way to cement grateful thinking into my daily routine.

- *Expressing gratitude to someone specific each day.* I have a goal each day of calling or sending a handwritten note of gratitude to at least one person I am grateful for and letting them know I appreciate them. This can also be done in person through my various daily encounters. This practice helps me cultivate a finer appreciation for the incredible people in my life.

- *Daily encounters filled with friendliness, kindness, and gratitude.* I am blessed to encounter dozens of people every week through my business and everyday life. My family and I engage with our church community each Sunday. We spend time with our friends. In all of these various encounters I have a wonderful opportunity with each person to be kind, positive, hopeful, and friendly and to express gratitude when appropriate. I hope I can positively contribute to a ripple effect that they will share with others through my actions.

Hopefully, after reading this short reflection, you will be more grateful for what you have that is good, but also for your *challenges*. Perhaps there are powerful lessons you have learned or difficult experiences that have shaped you for the better. I know my life is filled with these kinds of experiences! If nothing else, I encourage you to be grateful for simply being alive and for the opportunity to contribute to a more hopeful future. That would be a great place to start.

Grumpy or grateful . . . you have a choice!

Cultivate the habit of being grateful for every good thing that comes to you, and to give thanks continuously. And because all things have contributed to your advancement, you should include all things in your gratitude.

—Ralph Waldo Emerson

What is your current frame of mind? Grumpy? Grateful? Or something in between? How can you consistently get to a more grateful mindset? Practice the ideas in this chapter for two weeks and reflect on your progress.

CHAPTER 21

They Know I'm Catholic, Right?

I gave a talk one Sunday morning to the men's group of a large Atlanta Methodist church at the request of an old friend. When he asked me to speak to this group, months before the talk, I responded with a question that I asked him repeatedly every time we got together: "They know I'm Catholic, right?"

I engage one-on-one with people of other faiths (or no faith) almost every day and always enjoy the dialogue, but this was very different as I would be going on Protestant turf to deliver a talk. I allowed nagging self-doubt to creep in and began to regret my commitment the last few weeks leading up to the talk.

I speak to groups fairly often, and this should not have been a big deal, but speaking to a large group of Protestants was pushing me way out of my comfort zone. How would they respond? Would they ask me questions I couldn't answer? Would they start quoting Scripture and maligning the Church? What if they insulted the Blessed Mother? Would they criticize the Pope? What would I do?

My friend tried to reassure me with what he thought were encouraging words: "Don't worry, a lot of them are former Catholics." Good grief! Not only was I speaking as a Catholic in a Methodist church, but I was speaking to a group of former Catholics who had left the Church. It would be just my luck if everyone there had lingering issues they would love to take out on me.

My irrational sense of dread increased.

Then, I had an epiphany a few days before I spoke. I remembered three important things:

- *I needed to stop worrying and start praying.* I needed to give up my fear and anxiety to the Lord, trust in Him, and ask for strength and the guidance of the Holy Spirit.
- *This was an unbelievable opportunity to share the joy of my Catholic faith with my Christian brothers—many of whom were once Catholic.*
- *I knew my friend would not put me in a negative situation like the one my overactive imagination had cooked up.* I needed to have faith and trust in our friendship and his good intentions. I needed to avoid giving in to unfair stereotyping, which I would resent if it was directed at me.

Before I share with you what happened at the talk, let's take a brief time out and reflect a little on giving witness and ecumenical outreach to other Christian denominations. Do you recognize that I just illustrated the fear and anxiety many Catholics feel about sharing their faith? I have heard countless times that we must be cautious here in the "Protestant

South." We may get questions about the Blessed Mother or be asked why we have priests hear our confessions, or why we pray for the intercession of the saints. A fearful and insecure Catholic often becomes a *silent* Catholic, but Jesus expects more from us. If we only share our faith and witness with other Catholics—or worse, keep it to ourselves—how will the Church grow and spread Christ's message?

> "The harvest is plentiful but the workers are few. Ask the Lord of the harvest, therefore, to send out workers into his harvest field." (Matthew 9:37-38)

In my professional life, I encounter new people every day. Since my family and I joined the Church many years ago, I have been very open and transparent with others about my faith. In all of my numerous encounters with people of different faith backgrounds, I have had very few negative experiences. I generally find people to be curious about the Catholic Church, not adversarial. I am not naïve, and I recognize there are people who have strong negative feelings toward the Church, but they may be doing so out of misguided intentions, misunderstandings, or a lack of knowledge. We have a wonderful opportunity during these encounters to share the beautiful history of our two-thousand-year-old Church, dispel the rumors, and refute the myths. So many times in these conversations I have observed that we are more aligned than either of us realized and that often assumptions and incorrect information are the biggest barriers to agreement. But first, we must know our faith before we can explain it to anyone else.

Always be prepared to give an answer to everyone who asks you to give the reason for the hope that you have, but do it with gentleness and reverence, keeping your conscience clear, so that, when you are maligned, those who defame your good conduct in Christ may themselves be put to shame. (1 Peter 3:15-16)

Now, back to that talk at the Methodist church.

The prayers worked, and the Lord gave me the peace and strength I needed. The group could not have been more kind or welcoming. (Is there a lesson here for all of us?) I actually felt very comfortable when I got up to speak, and I trusted the Holy Spirit to convey the right words. I started out by sharing my faith journey into the Church before launching into a talk titled "Priorities and a Life Filled with Meaning" where I outlined my life priorities and the practical actions I was taking to ensure that I stayed on the right path. The audience heard quotes from saints and popes and lots of Scripture and *Catechism* references. I hoped they would see me as a father and husband struggling with the same things they did and recognize that keeping my focus on serving Christ and putting Him first in my life kept me on the right path. The audience applauded loudly when I finished, and many of them came up afterward to say that I really connected with them. Several asked for a copy of the talk, and many others asked if we could have coffee in the weeks ahead to discuss why I was so joyful about my Catholic faith as they were eager to learn more.

I didn't do anything extraordinary, and I am not the world's most amazing speaker. But the Holy Spirit worked through me, a Catholic, to connect with these good Protestant men in their church on a Sunday morning. We were simply Christian brothers from different faith traditions coming together to learn from one another.

Each of us will likely have numerous opportunities in our lifetimes to engage with people of different faiths or those with no faith at all. Perhaps all it takes is our willingness to share our joy, and a little courage, humility, transparency, and prayer to give a powerful witness. Are we willing to trust God and allow Him to work through us today?

Have you ever been nervous about sharing your faith or something else you deeply believed with people who have different perspectives and beliefs? How did you handle it? How were you received? What lessons from the experience have you carried with you into other areas of your life?

CHAPTER 22

Coffee, a Glass of Wine, and Lunch at a Thai Restaurant

Before the COVID-19 pandemic, I averaged two daily coffee meetings and a lunch with my clients and business network five days a week, and I had done this for more than twenty-five years. I largely built my network through this approach and truly looked forward to those daily encounters and deep conversations with clients, friends, and other business professionals. When the pandemic hit in 2020 and the world was turned upside down, we were forced into our home prisons, and nurturing relationships with our networks was not the top priority. As time passed and we understood better how to navigate through COVID-19, we embraced a mix of virtual connecting and meetings with safe-distancing and masks. Eventually, we have returned to a normal way of life as fear of the disease faded and our ability to combat and live with it dramatically increased.

I have intentionally *not* returned to my old habits of daily coffees and lunches with my network. I still work virtually 50 percent of the time as this is a more suitable fit for the confidential conversations my executive coaching and consulting work requires and the global makeup of my clients. I now connect with and nurture my network on a more selective in-person basis that works for my calendar and my desire for a healthier lifestyle, as these days I often get in a quick workout at noon.

This focus on fewer in-person conversations has surprisingly *increased* my enjoyment of the meetings and enhanced the quality of the conversations. Because of this narrower focus, I am more fully present and aware when I do meet with others, and I believe this reflects positively on the quality of my coaching conversations—and has led to a deeper investment in work, friend and family relationships, and my renewed passion for writing over the last few years. As a result of this shift, I have also increased the handwritten notes I send, random catch-up calls to friends and more frequently text or email to offer encouragement or just say hello to people in my network.

About six weeks before this book manuscript was finished, I had an interesting series of impactful in-person meetings over the course of one week that illustrates the power of this deeper focus on quality time with others.

A coffee meeting with a client prospect . . .

I had an early morning coffee meeting with a senior HR executive client prospect near his office. The HR leader reached out to me via LinkedIn and was interested in having me coach an executive on the senior leadership team of his company. We exchanged the usual back-and-forth questions about each other's backgrounds as we got to know each other. Halfway through the meeting, he asked me to send him a scope of work agreement to get started and with a smile said that I "came as advertised." I asked him what he meant, and he said I had helped his younger brother with his job search almost twenty years ago. His brother had been downsized from his company, and apparently, I was one of the only people who took the time to meet him, offer guidance, and make helpful introductions. His brother had remembered this kindness and encouraged his brother to reach out to me.

This reminded me of something my parents always taught me as a kid: "Always do the right thing. It will eventually come back to you, often in unexpected ways." Sometimes our little acts of kindness may come back to us like this unexpected client, and sometimes all we may receive is the quiet satisfaction that we did the right thing, which should always be payment enough.

A glass of wine with a good friend . . .

As an executive coach and someone who loves helping people, I brought this mindset with me as I met a good friend of mine for a drink the evening after the coffee meeting. We caught up with the latest family and work happenings while managing a few belly laughs, as this particular friend is great at poking fun at the absurdity of life. As the conversation continued, I found that it was my friend giving me great coaching and wise counsel, not the other way around. In the company of this trusted buddy I have known for almost twenty years, I found myself unburdening myself of things that were bothering me, the anxiety I was feeling about the current state of the world, and other obstacles I was working to overcome. *The coach had become the coachee.*

So often we may be struggling with burdens and stress we don't have to carry alone. How often do we let our guard down and allow friends and family members help us shoulder the load? I have struggled most of my life to allow others to help me as I detailed in chapter four, but every time I put my ego aside and seek help or receive it when it is kindly given, I feel an immediate sense of relief and gratitude.

Lunch at our favorite Thai restaurant . . .

The Friday of that same week, I had the opportunity to have lunch with my son, Alex. He lives at home with us, and he had been irritable that week and generally out of sorts. My wife and I were struggling to figure out why he was not himself when he asked me on Wednesday if we could do "something fun" together on Friday when he was off work. Alex rarely makes these requests, so I reorganized my schedule to be available.

We were able to play a round of putt-putt, which he loves, then head over to lunch at our favorite Thai restaurant. He seemed in a much better mood and more like himself as we ate our food. We had the usual conversations about favorite restaurants, our upcoming beach vacation, movies, and the Peloton workout he was doing that afternoon. I asked him near the end of our meal why he had been having a tough week, and he simply said, "I don't know. I just wanted to spend time with you."

In that short sentence, Alex addressed the problem in a

way that is often difficult for people on the autism spectrum to express. I was thankful I had been able to adjust my schedule to be present and address his desire for time with me. This may seem like a little thing to you, but how often do we miss these critical moments with loved ones and friends because of work or other priorities that are probably not as important as we think they are in the moment?

Being fully present in conversation is a gift to the person in front of you and a gift to yourself. It took a pandemic for me to adjust my meeting habits and focus on a deeper investment with fewer people and special weeks with meetings like the ones I just described to encourage me to stay on this path. I am grateful for everyone in my network, but as I get older, I desire the emphasis to increasingly be on more focused quality time and memorable moments.

Who will benefit from your focused attention this week? What might happen if you are open to and looking for surprising outcomes like the ones I shared in this chapter?

CHAPTER 23

A Silent Toast to an Empty Seat

An elderly man, who closely resembled the famous poet Robert Frost in his later years, sat in a booth diagonally across from me and one of my sons as we were enjoying our dinner on a warm Tuesday evening. There was something about this quiet, dignified older man dining alone that briefly intrigued me, but I quickly turned my attention back to the conversation I was having with my son. Several minutes went by before his dinner and a glass of wine arrived. Out of the corner of my eye, I saw him raise his glass with a trembling hand to make a silent toast to the empty seat in front of him.

I was struck by what I had just observed and quietly asked our server if she knew anything about the gentleman. She volunteered that he had been a frequent guest in the past with his wife. The server had heard that his wife had passed away, but she wasn't completely certain. She added that he had started coming back to the restaurant a few weeks ago after a long absence, always dining alone.

Not expecting to gain this depth of background and insight, I briefly pondered what he must have endured in losing his wife and wondered what kind of life they had built together. I thought of the special memories they had likely created . . . memories he must have been reminiscing over that prompted him to toast the empty place in front of him once occupied by his wife. I felt saddened and touched by all of this, but also challenged to continue doing my best to create special memories with my own wonderful wife and children—memories that would stay with me forever.

Moved by my brief experience over dinner, I asked the server for my check, but also for the check of the solitary gentleman. I felt a strong impulse to do something nice for this man. I anonymously paid for his meal and wrote a note at the top of the check: *Please enjoy a small act of kindness from one of your Roswell neighbors. I hope you have a wonderful evening.*

I did this to let this gentleman know he is not alone and to thank him in some small way. He will likely never know the impact he had on me over a meal, and our paths may not cross again, but he will know someone thought enough of him to share a simple act of kindness. Perhaps, for just a few moments, this made him feel a little less lonely in what can be an uncaring and cold world.

I left the restaurant with the timely reminder that life is precious and there are countless memories to be made. I have lost loved ones in my life and will inevitably deal with more loss in the years ahead; it's an unfortunate part of the human journey. I pray I do it with the same grace and dignity of this stranger. Going forward, I will commit to being more intentional about honoring with a silent toast those friends and loved ones who have left the world too soon and whose memories I will always cherish.

Who will receive your silent toast over dinner tonight?

CONCLUSION

Reflection, Journaling, Mining for Gold, and Other Helpful Ideas

In the Introduction, I shared with you at a high level how I define "being fully present." Among other observations, I offered an expected litany of best practices: eliminate distractions, actively listen, ask relevant questions, consider what you can learn, focus on how you can help, etc. These are all important and necessary, but now that you have read the stories in this book, I want to take you into a deeper exploration of this topic and how you might enhance your own practice of being fully present that will hopefully produce meaningful results.

As you ponder what you have been reading, you will see that many of the stories take place in relatively quiet places, such as in the woods during long walks or during prayer time. There was no multitasking, checking emails or texts, or thinking about upcoming meetings. All of the stories came to life and were memorialized in the absolute quiet of my comfortable home office where I love to reflect, write, and do my best work. We all would do well to spend more time in private quiet places that amplify distraction-free thinking and reflecting and less time in noisy public spaces and environments that over stimulate our brains and make it difficult to focus.

You have to show up and engage with people and life to truly enjoy the fruits of being fully present. Investing in new relationships, spending quality time with family and friends, going deeper with work colleagues and truly getting to know them—all this is foundational to being in a position to glean the kinds of lessons and epiphanies you read about in this book. It feels as if the world has gotten more introverted and siloed since the pandemic. I encourage all of us to make more of an effort to break out of the virtual world we have gotten so comfortable with and experience more in-person people interaction. Find the right balance for yourself. Virtual meetings are here to stay, and you can still practice being fully present in them, but they can never fully replace a handshake, a warm hug, or a life-changing conversation over a good meal.

I recognize that journaling is not for everyone, but I can't emphasize enough how helpful this practice has been for me when it comes to reflection and gleaning lessons from meetings, situations, or even distant memories. Every single story you read in this book began as notes in one of the two-dozen journals I have filled over the last twenty years. Because I practice daily reflection and intentional journaling, I consistently capture my thoughts and unpack lessons and ideas I have or may learn from others. I also glean from these writings how to make changes that allow me to show up more fully with others. It gave me great pleasure to pull out some of my older journals to find some of the stories you have read in this book. You may have a favorite app for this purpose or some other helpful approach, but please thoughtfully consider how helpful a simple, old-fashioned journal can be in elevating your ability to be fully present. By the way, taking notes *during* a meeting with someone is a powerful way to convey that you are fully present.

There is one helpful, overarching mindset and best practice I encourage you to adopt if you truly want to get the richest benefit from being fully present: *Always be mining for gold*. Recognize that every situation and encounter can offer great value to you or the other person, and it requires paying careful attention. Sometimes the "gold nuggets" come to us later, not in the moment. Reflecting on memories and seeking both the obvious epiphanies and hidden lessons, as you saw illustrated so often in this book, will change your life as you get more intentional with this practice. I do my best reflective "mining for gold" early in the morning over a quiet cup of coffee when I am sharpest and most alert.

I hope you will use the stories and ideas in this book to enhance your definition and practice of being fully present, and I hope this also helps you to embrace changes you may want to make in your life to help you grow and thrive. You will recognize that almost every experience and story in this book helped me in some way to be more aware of where I was at that moment in my life, what I needed to change, and the steps required to initiate the change. Not all encounters and situations will be positive on the surface, but adversity and difficulties can often be the most effective catalyst for teaching the most meaningful lessons.

I hope this book will inspire you and make you think. I hope it will be the catalyst for deeper reflection and an intentional focus on being fully present. Perhaps you will feel called one day, as I did, to write your own stories and share them with the world.

ACKNOWLEDGMENTS

Being Fully Present is not a book I intended to write. I was hard at work earlier this year on another business book that will be a follow up to 2021's *Essential Wisdom for Leaders of Every Generation* (look for a spring 2024 release) when the idea for *Being Fully Present* came to me during one of my frequent long walks in the woods. It occurred to me that over the years, I have had numerous encounters and experiences that caused me to think twice, learn powerful lessons, and even have an epiphany or two. Some of these stories have been captured in previous blog posts, many existed as entries in my journal, and others simply were fond memories. This book represents my humble attempt to share these stories that have meant so much to me with a wider audience.

First and foremost, I thank God for the life He has given me, for my wonderful family, and for the opportunity to do work I love every single day. The only viable explanation for the epiphanies and outcomes in many of the stories in this book are God at work . . . and I am truly humbled at the thought of the great love He has for all of us. All praise, honor and glory to Him! I am grateful to my wonderful wife, Sandra, for always being there for me and for her unwavering love and support. I would be lost without her. I am grateful for my sons, Alex and Ryan, and the daily privilege of being their father. Many of the experiences and lessons I shared in this book are the fruits of the life we have all made together, and I can't thank them enough.

No book is ever written in isolation. Our daily interactions with friends, family and even total strangers can sometimes leave lasting impressions that affect how we think, feel, and see the world. I would like to express my sincere gratitude to the people in my life, some of whom are mentioned in this book, who have had a profound impact on me.

I am very appreciative of Karen Daniel and our longstanding partnership and friendship, and for the book cover and interior art design for this book and others over the years. Thank you to Claudia Volkman for our literary partnership, your expert editing, and willingness to always challenge me when I need it.

To all who reviewed the book, offered helpful suggestions, and gave recommendations, please know that I am very appreciative of your time, wisdom, and thoughtfulness.

ABOUT THE AUTHOR

Randy Hain is the founder and president of Serviam Partners (ServiamPartners.com) and the co-founder of the Leadership Foundry (MyLeadershipFoundry. com). With a successful thirty-plus-year career in senior leadership roles, corporate talent, and executive search, he is a sought-after executive coach for senior leaders at some of the best-known companies in the United States who are seeking expert guidance on identifying and overcoming obstacles to their success or developing new leadership skills. He is also an expert at onboarding and cultural assimilation for senior leaders as well as helping senior leadership teams improve trust, clarity, collaboration, and candid communication. Randy also offers consulting and coaching for companies, teams, and individual business leaders looking to develop more authentic and effective business relationships both inside and outside their organizations. His deep expertise in business relationships is a true area of differentiation for him and Serviam Partners.

He is an active community leader and serves on the boards of organizations he cares about most. He is a longtime partner of the SEC (Southeastern Conference) Career Tour and presents on career readiness topics to the student-athletes and other leadership topics to leaders from the various SEC schools. As a member of the advisory board for the Brock School of Business at Samford University, Randy frequently presents on relevant business and career topics to the Samford students. He is passionate about promoting autism awareness and advocating for adults with autism in the workplace. He is also an active member of St. Peter Chanel Catholic Church. Randy has earned a reputation as a creative business partner and generous thought leader through his books, articles, and speaking engagements.

Randy is the award-winning author of nine other books, including *Upon Reflection: Helpful Insights and Timeless Lessons for the Busy Professional, Essential Wisdom for Leaders of Every Generation, Something More: The Professional's Pursuit of a Meaningful Life, LANDED! Proven Job Search Strategies for Today's Professional,* and *Special Children, Blessed Fathers: Encouragement for Fathers of Children with Special Needs,* all available on Amazon.

Learn more about Randy Hain's professional work, books, blog posts, and thought leadership at his website, www.ServiamPartners.com.

Made in the USA
Columbia, SC
20 October 2023

24725294R00074